Life in Colors

By George Boelcke:

The Colors of Leadership and Management

The Colors of Relationships

Colors Tools for Christians

The Colors of Sales and Customers

Colorful Personalities – Audio CD

It's Your Money! Tools, Tips and Tricks to Borrow Smarter and Pay It Off Quicker

The American Financial Nightmare CD

The Canadian Financial Nightmare CD

¡Quédese con Su Dinero! Los Secretos del Crédito y la Deuda

Life in Colors

*A guide to understanding
your children, your partner
and yourself*

George J. Boelcke, CCP

Educational
Development
Corporation

First edition 2011 by EDC Publishing,
A Division of Educational Development Corporation

Copyright © 2009 George J. Boelcke, CCP

For information contact:
EDC Publishing
P.O. Box 470663
Tulsa, OK 74147-0663
www.edcpub.com

George J. Boelcke
1183-14781 Memorial Dr. Houston, TX 77079
george@vantageseminars.com
www.vantageseminars.com

Colorful Personalities is a registered trademark of Vantage Consulting

Excerpt from *Marley and Me: Life and love with the world's worst dog* by John Grogan.
© 2005 by John Grogan. Reprinted by permission of HarperCollins Publishers.

Library of Congress Control Number: 2010936123

Printed and bound in the United States of America
1 2 3 4 5 6 7 8 9 10
ISBN: 978-1-60130-235-9

To:

Every attendee of the Colors seminars. To this day, no seminar is ever the same as another. Thank you for helping me to help others.

Thelma Box, whose Choices Seminar introduced me to Colors, and who keeps challenging others to follow their passions and living their purpose.

The thousands of consultants, supervisors, and others with Usborne Books and More who make such a powerful difference in the lives of so many families and children. Because if they didn't ... who would?

Ann Zitaruk – one of the few friends a Gold needs.

Table of Contents

The Colors Self-Assessment 11

Introduction. 15

The Beginning of Personality Typing 19

Blues: Relationships and Authenticity 23

Golds: Duty and Responsibility. 41

Oranges: Freedom and Skillfulness 61

Greens: Knowledge and Understanding 81

Our Combinations of Colors. 99

Relationships: Love is Colorblind. 119

The Colors of Children: Doing More of What Works 147

Self-esteem and Stress 204

The Last Word. 215

Additional Colors Self-Assessment. 222

The Colors Self-Assessment

On the next two pages is a short assessment, with an extra copy at the end of the book. It is important to remember that this is a self-assessment and not a test. There are no right or wrong answers, just groups of words designed to identify your own preferences, values, and priorities. It is not about how others would describe you, or how you might act in any specific situation, but rather about how you see yourself.

When you have completed the assessment, you will have a score in each of the different personality types, or Color groups. Your highest score will indicate your dominant personality type. The detailed sections of each chapter will describe your unique combinations of Colors identified by the assessment.

We are all combinations of the Colors. Think of each of them as pieces of a jigsaw puzzle; all four play an integral part in making each of us a complete person.

Our uniqueness comes from the different sizes of these pieces – the combinations of our total score. Some people will have all four Colors in balance, but most of us tend to have one or two scores much higher than the others. There is no better or worse – only different, as each Color is equally valuable and special.

Let the journey begin …

The Colors Self-Assessment

Score each group of words, for all eight questions, on a scale of:

    4 – which is the most like you

    3 – which is quite a bit like you

    2 – which is a little bit like you

    1 – which is the least like you

(Each question can have only one score of 1, one 2, one 3 and one 4.)

1. a) _____ compassion, sharing, sympathetic

  b) _____ duty, detailed, traditions

  c) _____ verbal, risk-taker, promoter

  d) _____ rational, knowledge, visionary

2. a) _____ feelings, meaningful, cooperation

  b) _____ conservative, reliable, stability

  c) _____ spontaneous, generous, action

  d) _____ credibility, focused, probing

3. a) _____ authentic, encouraging, spiritual

  b) _____ devoted, cautious, status quo

  c) _____ surprises, freedom, shortcuts

  d) _____ inventive, principled, competence

4. a) _____ unique, sensitive, peacemaker

  b) _____ steady, planning, loyal

  c) _____ open-minded, playful, hands-on

  d) _____ curious, determined, rational

5. a) ____ tender, involved, connecting
   b) ____ lists, procedural, responsible
   c) ____ competitive, outgoing, direct
   d) ____ exploring, skeptical, complex

6. a) ____ devoted, caring, self-improvement
   b) ____ dependable, structured, belonging
   c) ____ flexible, daring, persuasive
   d) ____ independent, perfectionist, reserved

7. a) ____ intuition, sharing, positive
   b) ____ orderly, honor, rule-follower
   c) ____ immediate, skillful, active
   d) ____ theoretical, calm and cool, learning

8. a) ____ affectionate, accommodating, harmony
   b) ____ private, serious, moral
   c) ____ networking, adventure, winning
   d) ____ analytical, logical, improving

Your total score for:

a) Blue ____ b) Gold ____ c) Orange ____ d) Green ____

(The total of your four scores will equal 80.)

Introduction

Welcome to our journey of discovery – a journey into understanding and appreciating one another. By celebrating our differences, we gain new insights which help us see, value and interact with each other. This is a book about all of us – a guide to better understanding ourselves, our partners and co-workers, our parents, and our children.

Let's face it, every day we meet and interact with many people who are very different from us. They don't think like us. They make decisions way too quickly, or they seem to take forever to make up their minds. Some want to have fun all the time, and they find it challenging dealing with others who seldom relax and let loose. There are people who often just blurt things out and appear oblivious to the fact that they've really hurt other people's feelings. There are some people who want to tell you how their watch was made, when you just want to know what time it is.

*"Things can go horribly wrong when you
don't understand each other."*
Canon Ad

Different is never about being unlovable or bad. Different is not about better or worse; it is only that – different. It is simply that not everyone shares our personality type. Every Color sees the world through a different set of glasses, providing each Color with its own definition of family, organization, honesty, fun, competition – a unique vision of the world. And each of our four Colors communicates, acts, thinks, talks, and functions in its own way within that world.

Discovering the power of Colors results in many "Aha!" moments. Imagine how much richer and more stress-free our lives would be if we had a way to easily understand what makes others tick. What if we could truly understand other people's values, strengths, and stresses? What if we spent more time looking for what we have in common, and used our energies to create understanding and common bonds instead of passing judgment? What if we could learn to see through other Colors' glasses?

*To have some different results you
have to do some different things.*

This journey of discovery is in large part about yourself. It begins with acknowledging and explaining your own talents, joys, and actions, and also your stresses – those you have always felt, but perhaps could not always define or explain. The insights of Colors will open your heart and your mind to truly understanding yourself and others in ways you never thought possible, and in ways you will utilize for a lifetime.

Personality types and the study of human behavior is not an exact science. We are always limited to general preferences and common denominators. Throughout this book, the words *majority, often, tend to, prefer, largely,* and so on, are used to clearly emphasize that insights into, and understanding of, human behaviors and our different personality types, is not about right or wrong, or black or white.

Personality types are also never meant to stereotype or pigeonhole. They are not about putting people into categories or labeling them. It might be easy to label, but it would be as wrong as it would be pointless. As one of almost seven billion people in the world, every one of us is unique and special. Yet within our personality types, we share a vast array of common behaviors, strengths, and stresses.

The true value of the tools and insights of Colors comes in using this new understanding and applying that knowledge in real life, every day. Just as no one has ever learned to drive a car simply by reading the manual, growth in understanding ourselves and others involves an active, participatory and continuous journey.

The insights of Colors is one-half awareness and one-half choosing to value others for who they are, instead of wanting them to be more like ourselves.

Persons are Gifts

Persons are gifts of God to me. They are already wrapped. Some beautifully and others less attractively. Some have been mishandled in the mail, others come "special delivery," some are loosely wrapped, and others very tightly enclosed. But the wrapping is not the gift and this is an important realization. It is so easy to make a mistake in this regard, to judge the contents by the cover. Sometimes the gift is opened very easily; sometimes the help of others is needed.

Maybe it is because they are afraid to look inside my wrapping. Maybe I don't trust my own contents. Or it may be that I have never fully accepted the gift that I am. Every meeting and sharing of persons is an exchange of gifts.

My gift is Me; your gift is You. We are gifts to each other.

Author unknown

Chapter One

The Beginning of Personality Typing

From the beginning, the human race has been blessed with a wealth of talents and diverse abilities, including our abilities to think, reason, learn, and grow. Along with these comes our thirst for knowledge and our pursuit of understanding.

Long ago, learning was mainly about physical survival, but as communities grew and developed, and populations expanded, it became clear that each individual had different talents and abilities, some learned, others inherent in personality. What also became clear was the need to interact and get along with one another. Since that time, people have been studying and searching for ways to create an understanding and appreciation for our different gifts, generally recognizing four different groups or types.

The first study of personality types dates back to the ancient Greek physician Hippocrates, around 400 BC. Hundreds of years later, astrologers began using the four elements of nature – earth, water, air, and fire – to define and classify different personalities. The First Nations people also believed that our natural world was created in groups of four and developed their Medicine Wheel as a powerful healing tool divided into four Spirit Keepers.

In modern times, the Swiss psychologist and psychiatrist Carl Jung refined the study of personality types. Jung's studies showed him repeated behaviors which he identified as four distinct ways of dealing with the world. He suggested that parents, society, and the environment play only a small role in determining these ways. Jung believed that fundamentally, individuals were already born with their natural personality types or functions, which he defined as *sensing, thinking, feeling,* and *intuiting.*

Using Jung's theories, Katharine Briggs completed many years of further research on the same subject. She shared Jung's belief that the many, and seemingly random, behaviors humans exhibit were actually very orderly and identifiable and could be categorized. Along with her daughter, Isabel Myers-Briggs, she developed the Myers-Briggs Type Indicator™(MBTI), published in 1956, which classified temperament characteristics into sixteen specific types. Significant research and testing has proven its validity over many years. Its success and broad application greatly increased interest in personality and temperament theory, and is still widely used today.

Dr. David Keirsey, a clinical psychologist, refined the work of Myers-Briggs in 1978. Using the MBTI and the theories of Carl Jung, Keirsey returned to the basics of classifying personalities into four base temperaments. He published his work in the widely-read book, *Please Understand Me.*

Another step was the development of True Colors™ in 1979. David Keirsey was a mentor to a California teacher named Don Lowry. Lowry used simple language to describe the four distinct personality types for use in the school system. His goal was to translate the very complex psychological material into everyday language – and he succeeded. In fact, the introduction is sometimes presented as a stage production using actors to portray the four personality types.

One of the first uses of colors as a psychological test was developed in 1947 by Dr. Max Luscher, a Swiss psychologist. Luscher used four basic colors and four auxiliary colors in his assessments. His four base colors consisted of Blue as a calming color, Green to symbolize strong will, Red as an energy color, and Yellow to represent achievement and future orientation.

From ancient times until today, the symbolism and use of colors has been associated with everything from marketing and behavior descriptions to interior decorating. Blue is the color of the sky and the seas. It is a color of warmth, representing calm and harmony. Orange is a much more vibrant and brighter color and can symbolize "look at me," or exude energy and action. Gold is the color of one of the most desired metals. Expressions such as "The gold standard," or, "Good as gold," imply stability, tradition, and dependability. Finally, Green is nature's primary color and very much connected to thoughts of growth, abundance, and creativity.

For simplicity and ease of use, describing our personality types in terms of these four Colors is one of the most effective and user-friendly methods.

The power of understanding Colors yields a vastly improved communication tool and the gift, or at least the option, of seeing people in a different light. Something so simple really can become a powerful tool to impact lives and relationships in practical and measurable ways.

Understanding and communicating with other
Colors in ways they value comes with huge rewards
for both them and you. It allows you to do more of what
works, and less of what doesn't, in all of your relationships.

Don't get your feelings hurt. This is a positive. I'm going to teach you to stand up for yourself and learn to say no, Thompson!

We've done all the tests, but when she says "Code Blue" she's definitely not referring to a medical condition.

Chapter Two

Blues: Relationships and Authenticity

The drive to put their hearts into anything
they are passionate about.

The focus to help others less fortunate than themselves.

Appreciating beauty without analysis.

A classic line: *"Winning isn't everything – harmony is."*

A great quote: *"The best and most beautiful things
in the world cannot be seen or even touched.
They must be felt within the heart."*
Helen Keller

*I believe that my most important goal in life is to touch others and
to contribute in making this a better world for us all. I am unique
and authentic. I value my relationships and reach out to others
through my warmth, compassion, and caring. I am an idealist
and quite intuitive. I look for unity and harmony and love
teamwork. I am passionate in my caring and sharing with others
in order to help them realize their dreams and unlimited potential,
and I value playing a small part in helping them grow.*

Blues are the relationship experts of the world. With warm smiles,
soft voices, and frequent eye contact, they make everyone around them
feel special and included. Their approachable, friendly manner and
helpful nature easily draw others in. In any new group, Blues quickly and
easily connect with others with their warm and caring ways.

It is not uncommon for Blues to spend large parts of their day helping friends, co-workers, or clients by listening to their needs and truly feeling their pain. Seldom will they say no, refuse to lend a hand, or make their work more important than their friends' needs. One of the big questions in life is whether someone is a giver or a taker. If the question has been asked about Blues, then the answer is easy.

Caring and Being Cared About

Blues naturally see the good in everyone and everything, making them excellent caregivers, mediators, and team players. Caring for others and trying to make the world a better – and a softer – place are two powerful ways in which Blues make their unique contributions to others' lives. They will always turn their spare time into time-to-spare, asking themselves, "If I don't, who will?"

Encouraging and supporting others is a total win-win for Blues, who know that the best way to make a friend is to be a friend. When Blues help others to succeed, they do so because to them, it is simply the right thing to do. They intuitively know just what to say to encourage, cheer up and support whoever needs it.

Sometimes – many times – that unconditional caring and love is hard to find in return. Yet for Blues, it is both valuable and critical. It is the primary reason most Blues have, or would love to have, a pet. Blues know their pets love them unconditionally and teach them so much about life. In his bestselling book, *Marley and Me*, author John Grogan describes this Blue mind-set in such a powerful way:

> *Was it possible for a dog to point humans to the things that really matter in life? Loyalty, courage, devotion, simplicity, joy? And the things that did not matter, too.*

Status symbols mean nothing to him. A dog judges others not by their color or creed or class but by who they are inside. Give him your heart and he will give you his. And yet we as humans, so much wiser and more sophisticated, have always had trouble figuring out what really counts and what does not.

Communication Is Not Just the Talking Part

All Blues are gifted communicators, but they prefer meaningful, one-on-one conversations. They appreciate the chance to share their dreams and ideas in a safe environment, where they will not be laughed at or judged. In conversations, they ask sincere, open-ended questions in order to get to know someone. When Blues ask how we are, they really do want to know. And when they wish us a great day, they really do mean it.

A smile or a kind word costs nothing,
yet says so much and has such great value.

In conversation, Blues are very active listeners. They maintain frequent eye contact and often mirror the other person's emotions with their facial expressions. Where others might understand our pain, Blues will actually feel it, always willing to share a laugh or a good cry with us. In any office or group situation, Blues will always know everything there is to know about their team members. They will always know because Blues listen while other people just hear. They observe while others simply watch.

If you ask Blues whether they would prefer an e-mail, a call, or a get-together for coffee, almost all will pick the get-together. Blues understand that relationships cannot be built by e-mail. Getting together with someone allows them to use their intuition and empathy and to really listen and get to know someone.

In return, when Blues want to talk, they are only asking for others to listen – not to fix or to solve, but only to listen with an open heart and mind. Just this simple, yet powerful act will make any Blue person feel special and cared for.

Just Listen

When I ask you to listen to me and you start to give me advice, you have not done what I asked. When I ask you to listen and you begin to tell me why I should not feel that way, you are trampling on my feelings. When I ask you to listen to me and you feel you have to do something to solve my problem, you have failed me – strange as it may seem.

Listen. All I asked was that you listen, not talk or do or fix, just hear me and I can do for myself; I am not helpless – maybe discouraged and faltering, but not helpless. When you do something for me that I can and need to do for myself, you contribute to my fear and weakness.

But when you accept as a simple fact that I do feel what I feel no matter how irrational, then I can quit trying to convince you and get to the business of understanding what is behind this irrational feeling. And when that's clear, the answers are obvious and I don't need advice. Irrational feelings make sense when we understand what's behind them. So, please listen and just hear me. And, if you want to talk, wait a minute for your turn; and I will listen to you.

— Author unknown

Living in Their Hearts

Blues ride a lifelong roller coaster of emotions. They succeed by following their intuition because for them, feelings are just as valid in decision-making as logic. Everything – information, feedback, and what they observe – goes straight to their hearts.

All of their lives, Blues have known that their hearts hold information their heads do not. Blues live by their feelings and draw on their emotional intuition in the decision-making process. This is something other Colors have trouble understanding and appreciating. But Blues can get off-track when they don't follow their intuition. That intuition is their compass, and they should use it, even if it can be a challenge to explain their motivations or put their feelings into words.

There are times, however, when Blues wish they had an off switch for those feelings. Blues will readily admit that their feelings are easily hurt, and there are many occasions when their hearts are broken and their sadness lingers. But is a Blue's broken heart only a metaphor, something for country music and romance novels?

According to a report from Johns Hopkins University, there may be more to it than that. In a research study, physicians examined a group of mostly older women who had developed serious heart problems after experiencing a sudden emotional shock. None of the women had previously suffered a heart attack, and very few of the participants even had mild symptoms of heart disease prior to the emotional event.

The research physicians discovered that a group of stress hormones, which included adrenalin, was present in the women after the event, at up to 34 times greater levels than normal. On average, two to three times higher than the levels reached during a heart attack! According to cardiologist Dr. Ilan Wittstein, at least 25 percent of the women in the study would have died without medical intervention.

Doctors cannot understand how, or why, women's hearts appear to be more vulnerable to emotional shock than men's. While doctors might not be able to explain it, could the fact that the vast majority of Blues are females be one reason? After all, what the mind suppresses, the body expresses.

Countless Blues (and also many Golds) often find themselves experiencing physical symptoms of stress, hurt, anger and burnout, particularly when they suppress feelings and frustrations to avoid conflict. For Blues, buried feelings never die, and no matter what others say, time does not heal all wounds.

The Value of a Hug

Blues would much rather receive a genuine hug than a handshake. In relationships, Blues look for both quality and quantity time with their partner. In his bestselling book, *The Five Love Languages*, author Gary Chapman describes five distinct languages everyone speaks when showing or receiving affection. Two of these love languages are physical touch and spending quality time together, both of which are critical to Blues.

Holding hands and receiving hugs are the natural ways Blues' feelings of being cared for and loved are validated. They are also the ways in which Blues share their affection, connecting through a soft touch on the shoulder, a warm handshake, or a caring hug. How sad then, that these are becoming less acceptable and more politically incorrect:

> *It seemed innocent enough, and was actually very moving at the time. But it took a different turn after five-year-old Savanna was seen giving her friend Sarah a hug on the playground of their pre-school. Savanna's parents were called into the office*

to "deal" with this matter. But it was not because either
Savanna or her friend thought it was inappropriate or because
either set of parents had an issue with it. Hugging was simply
against the rules and broke school policy.

Whether the school's policy is right or wrong, whether it is reasonable or not, two more children have learned that hugs, for connecting with and comforting others, are wrong. At school or at work, in church or with friends, every day Blues look for ways to make their world a little softer and more caring. And they hug. Because for Blues, a hug is a handshake with meaning and feelings.

Making a Difference

Blues seek to create a better world, to leave this world a better place then they found it. They make up a large number of environmentalists. They also support countless charities with their time, money, and talents. Blues are some of the most active volunteers, generally working behind the scenes in small groups, almost always in an organization that has a strong people or animal connection. While their interests vary widely, from breast cancer research to the Humane Society, to their local church, Blues will always be active in a cause they are passionate about, where they feel they can make a difference.

Blues take countless journeys of personal growth and self-discovery, and they look to motivate and inspire others along the way. Because they are gifted with extraordinary communication skills, creativity and expressive natures, many Blues are drawn to careers in the media, where they are able to reach and to help vast numbers of people, making a difference in a measurable way.

Rachael Ray is the host of a number of cooking shows on the Food Network. While a cooking show isn't a news flash, Ray has become a media darling in the U.S., where Blues are only around 12% of the population.

As a relatively small Colors group, few people understand the values and gifts of Blues, which has made Ray the target of many media questions wondering how she always finds a way to look at the positives of every issue, or how she could possibly be so cheerful, helpful, and upbeat all the time. For years, Ray has been the subject of many judgmental comments and stories. Surely, someone "that nice" must either be putting on an act, or simply be phony. How sad, totally false, and very hurtful to question any Blue's motives and drive.

During her show Ray actually serves food to the audience herself and has a natural gift of making people feel welcome and included. Her style on the show is to chat and to genuinely connect with people without lecturing. Even outside the studio, Ray is totally accessible to her fans, loves to hug, and chooses to focus her show more around her guests, instead of celebrities. There is no teleprompter, earpiece, or cue card. She doesn't even have writers for the show – just Ray and her ability to simply be herself.

Another well-known media star who seems true Blue and is making a difference in the lives of millions of viewers is Oprah Winfrey. Oprah stands head and shoulders above other television hosts when she shares her gift for connecting whole-heartedly with her viewers and her guests. When Oprah displays emotions and speaks from her heart, it is absolutely genuine. For this Blue role model, just like for all Blues, it almost impossible to be phony or insincere.

Oprah is just one well-known example of the millions of Blues who combine their eternal optimism with their dreams of making a real difference in the world. Even the theme of the talk show she hosts, *change your life television*, reflects her passion and purpose: making a positive impact on the lives of others.

In 2003, Oprah shared an even bigger dream: to help one million children in Africa. While that number seemed unrealistic to most people, Blues believe in dreaming the impossible dream. And this seemingly unreachable goal became reality in January of 2007, when Oprah opened The Leadership Academy for Girls, in South Africa. The school will eventually be able to accommodate 450 girls each year. Remember, never bet against a Blue person who has a purpose, dream, or passion.

This wonderful story truly describes a life lived with purpose and meaning. But it's not just about Oprah. Many Blues have turned their own dreams and passions into reality; they just have not received the attention or publicity. In fact, for most Blues, attention is more of an embarrassment than a motivator.

Giving in to the Needs of Others

As peacemakers and peacekeepers, Blues often go along in order to get along. Blues have a tendency to bend to the wishes of others and to the will of a group. They never want to appear selfish. Learning to stand up for their own needs and wants is a difficult challenge. That inability to say no and to set boundaries seems strange to other Colors, who can't understand why Blues frequently sacrifice their own wishes and desires to accommodate others, to fit in, or to feel included.

The Blue tendency to give in and go along can make it difficult for others to notice when Blues are hurting, even when an emotional outburst is imminent. The overwhelming desire Blues have to take care of others can leave them feeling that standing up for their own needs is selfish, so they seldom express their own wants or priorities. This makes it critical that other Colors be particularly sensitive to the needs and feelings of their Blue friends.

In order to avoid conflict, Blues frequently talk around the point and have no trouble sugarcoating a difficult issue. Yet they are appreciative of other Colors' ability to communicate in more direct and specific ways. Blues do need to learn to communicate more clearly – to tell it like it is. After all, helping someone does not mean telling them what they want to hear, but caring enough to be honest with them – for Blues, something that's easier said than done.

It's the Little Things

Success for Blues is about making a difference and doing something simply because it needs doing. Blues want to feel that they have an impact. Payday is about hearing how they have made a difference in the lives of others. And best of all is when this feedback is received one-on-one and in person, not through applause, reviews, or a group thank-you.

Throughout their lives, Blues are the least likely Color to choose a career or job for the money. Of course their financial needs are no different than anyone else's, but money is seldom one of their primary motivators. "Can I make a difference here?" and, "Will I feel included and be part of a team?" are much more important questions. They can also be deal-breakers. Having more money is great, but the Blue focus is on what the money will allow them to accomplish. For Blues, passionate about a career or a project, a little piece of their heart goes into everything they do; they don't go through the motions without emotions.

Even when a Blue sends a card or a note, there is almost always a little something extra. It might be a sticker, a drawing on the envelope, or something tucked inside. It is not just a card – it's a Blue making a personal connection. The challenge for Blues' friends, families and co-workers is to understand and acknowledge the little touches and special ways.

> *"Don't look for big things, just do*
> *small things with great love."*
> Mother Teresa

When Feelings Can Get in the Way

Blues are deeply affected by criticism, harsh words, and cruelty. Their strong desire for peace and harmony has a price: It makes Blues extra sensitive to any conflict or injustice. These misunderstandings and inequities go against their nature and create significant stress. Blues often interpret criticism as a personal attack – they take things personally no matter the intention or how carefully worded.

In these instances, Blues will forgive, but will seldom forget. They may become quieter, withdrawn, and resentful, but these might be the only clues that they're upset and hurt. The other person likely has no idea how the Blue is feeling. Yet with no outlet or resolution, Blues will continue to avoid conflict, choosing not to make waves or speak up, even if they may be dying inside. Sometimes – many times – other Colors really do need to listen to what Blues are *not* saying.

Blues cannot tell their heart what to think, and there is no on-off switch for their feelings. Helping others is a great way Blues build their self-esteem, and they never stop to wonder what's in it for them. Yet Blues can get caught in a cycle of wondering what else, or what more, they could have done, instead of focusing on the huge positive impact they actually make. Too, often, and almost always incorrectly, they take on someone else's failure as their own.

Teamwork Makes the Dream Work

Blues are driven to create genuine relationships and harmony, and they are particularly gifted in their ability to work as part of a group or a team. Always sensitive to the needs of others, Blues make great team-builders, helping everyone feel special and part of the group. They are strong believers in fostering an environment of inclusion, and they work tirelessly to create a positive and supportive atmosphere. Blues truly believe that we can do anything, and that we can achieve great things if we just work together.

This fall, when you see geese heading south for the winter flying along in 'V' formation, you might consider what science has discovered as to why they fly that way.

FACT: As each bird flaps its wings, it creates an 'uplift' for the bird immediately following. By flying in a 'V' formation, the whole flock has at least 71% greater flying range than if each bird flew on its own.

LESSON: People who share a common direction and sense of community can get where they are going more quickly and easily because they are traveling on the thrust of one another.

FACT: When a goose flies out of formation, it suddenly feels the drag and resistance of trying to go it alone. It quickly gets back into formation to take advantage of the lifting power of the bird in front of it.

LESSON: If we have as much common sense as a goose, we stay in formation with those headed where we want to go. We are willing to accept their help and give our help to others. It is harder to do something alone than together.

FACT: When the lead goose gets tired, it rotates back into the formation and another goose flies to the point position.

LESSON: It is sensible to take turns doing the hard and demanding tasks and sharing leadership. As with geese, people are interdependent of each others' skills, capabilities and unique gifts, talents, or resources.

FACT: The geese flying in formation honk from behind to encourage those up front to keep up their speed.

LESSON: We need to make sure our honking is encouraging. In groups where there is encouragement, the production is much greater. The power of encouragement (to stand by one's heart or core values and encourage the heart and core of others) is the quality of honking we seek. We need to make sure our honking is encouraging and not discouraging.

FACT: When a goose gets sick, wounded or shot down, two other geese will drop out of formation with that goose and follow it down to lend help and protection. They stay with the fallen goose until it dies or is able to fly again. Then they launch out on their own, or with another formation, to catch up with their flock.

LESSON: If we have the sense of a goose, we will stand by our colleagues and each other in difficult times as well as in good.

– From a speech by Angeles Arrien and based upon
  the original research of the naturalist Milton Olson.

Since Blues draw significant energy and purpose from being part of a group, working in isolation can make them feel as if they're being punished. Blues truly love to be included and to feel that they are needed. Their desire to be part of a team shows in their strong ability to share both the work and the credit. Blues avoid being the star or the center of attention, and any recognition they receive is readily shared amongst their team. But as they clearly put people before tasks, Blues admit that staying focused and organized, or making paperwork a priority, can be a real challenge at times.

What Not to Say?

In the heat of discussion, or when making a decision, Blues want others to understand how passionate, important, and serious something is. Whether with a co-worker, friend, or partner, there are two statements which hinder a resolution with Blues:

Whatever you want. Usually motivated by the desire to extricate themselves from the situation and to end the discussion and get back to whatever they were doing, this is always the wrong thing to say to Blues. Blues feel that this response means their argument is not important, and is not being heard or valued. For better or worse, Blues look to others for opinions, answers and validation. They need to know that their co-worker, partner or friend really does care and really is listening. Perhaps other Colors are wishing Blues would just stop talking about an issue, but they are going about it the wrong way and making things worse. Blues will often talk until they feel they have been heard, and cutting them off will not help achieve that goal.

You are overreacting. Wrong. Blues' feelings do run deep, and it is more than likely that they are truly passionate about the issue.

Perhaps their strong intuition is guiding them, or maybe their feelings are hurt. Maybe no one is "getting it," or understanding how important, or hurtful, something is. Yes, small things do sometimes get blown out of proportion in a Blue argument, but "you are overacting," is not the best way to help a Blue realize that.

What You See and Hear from Blues

Blues are open and caring, warm and friendly, and they have a natural way of connecting with others. Blues have pictures of family and pets around the office, probably on their fridge, and throughout the house. Their facial expressions are animated, and they are very active listeners with a gift for getting others to open up and share.

Blues express lots of emotions in their voices and often use feeling-type words. They use humor and laughter in conversation and ask many open-ended questions to encourage others to express themselves. Blues really want to get to know someone and show lots of empathy when speaking. Others quickly notice their soothing voices and calm, welcoming, and enthusiastic tones. Blues seek to smooth things over and often say *I'm sorry*, even when they are not at fault.

Now I Understand…

You give and give and can frequently run on empty. I need to learn to be sensitive to your needs and be aware that you have a hard time saying no. You are a loyal friend, a great partner, someone I love spending time with. You keep dreams and possibilities alive and always look for the good and the positive in everyone and everything.

I understand that when you talk I don't need to fix. I just need to listen in the same caring way that you always do. Not judging, not fixing, and not being critical – just listening. Because you open your heart so often, so easily, I need to always be mindful to step gingerly.

I want to help you choose ways to take care of yourself. After all, it is only when you take care of yourself that you can take care of others.

Almost everything you do has a little piece of your heart in it. A little part of you is in every project and conversation and in all other areas of your life. You value putting your heart into everything you truly believe in.

You have intuition. You listen to it and follow it, and you are right more often than not. It also means I don't have to put on an act; I can always be myself because you will not reject the real me.

I marvel at your ability to connect with others so easily in spiritual and meaningful ways. You don't just define the word friendship – you live it through your words and actions every day, all day.

Finally, I will remember that your hug or a warm touch cures many things and touches others in special, caring ways.

I am your boss or your friend. I am your partner, someone you work with, or your relative ... and now I understand you a little better.

Common Blue Strengths

Authenticity
Cares for others
Creative
Devoted
Empathetic
Flexible
Friendly
Good listener
Honest
Intuitive
Like to laugh ... and cry
Loyal
Positive, eternal optimist
Sincere, genuine
Spiritual
Tactful
Totally people-oriented
Won't let others down

Brings joy to others
Compassionate
Democratic
Easy going
Sees potential in everyone
Forgiving
Generous
Great hugger
Wants to include everyone
Kind hearted
Loving and romantic
Peacemaker
Sensitive
Smoothes things over
Sympathetic
Team-builder
Trustworthy

Common Blue Stressors

Arguments
Inability to say no, burnout
Conflict, disharmony
Deadlines
Feeling they haven't done enough
Inflexibility in others
Humorless people
No eye contact
Not being taken seriously
Lack of empathy or hugs from others
People without integrity
Giving and receiving criticism
Inability to save the world
When work comes before people

Attempting to please everyone
Cold people
Criticism and harsh tone/voice
Domineering people
Hurt feelings
Office politics
Lack of romance
Silent treatment
Not making time for oneself
Paperwork
Phony people/pushy salespeople
Feeling unappreciated
Worrying about others' problems

I can understand how losing your to-do list is stressful. But you'll make a new one by tomorrow at the latest, I promise.

Maybe we will be off this island by Friday. It's great that you're always so reliable, but was it really necessary to kill the cell phone battery cancelling your appointments?

Chapter Three

Golds: Duty and Responsibility

The drive to plan the work and work the plan.

The focus on finishing one thing at a time before moving on.

A classic line: *"I know I'm right – it's either black or white."*

A great quote:
From the biggest deals to the smallest details,
Golds will always take care of it.

I believe in following through on commitments and showing others that I am a dependable, prepared, and punctual person. I am very loyal and have a strong sense of right and wrong. I value my home, my family, and our traditions. I am a faithful and caring friend. Helping others is important to me and engenders a sense of belonging. I plan things out properly and follow orderly and concrete steps to see things through to completion.

Golds are the largest Color group and seem to take the workload of the world on their shoulders. Whether they have been asked to or not, the way Golds see it, if somebody needs to do it, it might as well be them. *If it is to be, it's up to me.*

Their strong sense of duty makes Golds some of the most loyal friends and the largest number of volunteers. In fact, Golds and Blues make up more than two-thirds of all volunteers. Giving back and lending a hand are great self-esteem builders, but apart from that, volunteering is just the right and proper thing to do.

Whatever the task or commitment, Golds will make sure it is completed in a professional, businesslike manner without fanfare. They are often impatient to get started, much preferring to move forward rather than sitting around talking about it.

Golds are supportive, trustworthy and dedicated to their relationships. They are also some of the most loyal employees, the kind who would give two week's notice even if they won the lottery. Golds draw a large sense of purpose and identity from their work, whether that work is as a stay-at-home parent, an employee of someone else, or as a volunteer. Golds need to feel needed – they look for that sense of belonging to give them a real purpose in life.

Like a Rock

Golds take their responsibilities very seriously. Their word is their bond, and they will go through fire to make sure they keep it. No excuses and no cop-outs – no matter what. It might overload them, and perhaps they should say no, but that's a lesson difficult for Golds to learn. When Golds give their word, they honor it, no matter what.

Advertisers focus a large part of their marketing research on demographics and personality types since it allows them to effectively target a specific audience. Expressions such as, *as good as gold, solid as a rock, rock solid,* or *like a rock* accurately describe the mind-set of Golds.

Chevrolet, for example, describes its trucks as long-lasting and dependable. However, there are many more adjectives and phrases, either expressed or implied, in their advertisements which also resonate with Golds: *solid, steady, not going to let you down, reliable, there for you, count on me, true to my word, tough, stable,* and many more.

Mark agreed to help out with a school fundraiser for his daughter. It was not the best timing in his busy life, but his strong sense of obligation made it difficult to say no when he was asked. Yet halfway through the project, it seemed as though most of the committee had abandoned Mark. With his Gold reluctance to ask for help, more and more of the work landed on his shoulders. After all, he had given his word to chair the committee and he would see it through. The event was going to be a success and it WOULD get done on time, on budget, and raise the money the group had set as their goal. None of those were optional, and neither Mark, nor any Gold, would accept any excuses, quit on the project, or refuse to take on the additional work in order to make it happen.

The project was becoming quite stressful and more and more like a full-time job. But there was a job to do and he was going to honor the commitment and keep his word. Of course, the fundraiser went incredibly well. All the details were taken care of, the evening ran smoothly, and Mark felt on top of the world, yet totally run down and tired.

The Never-ending To-do List

Golds love making lists – everywhere and for every occasion. Lists are an ever-present reminder, a guide to what still needs to be accomplished, and an essential tool for success. Ask most Golds what they would do if they remembered something after they had gone to bed, and most will tell you they'd get up and make a quick note (many will keep paper and pens in their night table). Such is their unwavering sense of responsibility, that if they did not make a note, they probably would not be able to relax or fall asleep. They would simply lie there thinking, "don't forget, don't forget …"

Gold joy though, does not come from adding to a list; satisfaction comes from crossing everything off! Turning a to-do list into a done list, that is the Gold definition of fun. When they are in control of scheduling, life runs pretty smoothly. Where the Gold stress level increases is when unexpected tasks appear, or when they are asked to make changes to set plans or routines.

This mind-set makes Golds highly efficient, if not always very flexible. Should their spouses need help, a Gold may ask them to wait until they have finished cleaning up the garage (or whatever project is on the list for today). Before a meeting, Golds want to know what will be discussed, who has the agenda, and who will make sure the meeting ends on time. And, if their credit card bill arrives in the mail today, it will get paid tonight or tomorrow. True, it may not be due for another week, but paying it means one more thing crossed off the list.

To stay focused and remain efficient, Golds look for options, and they value a bottom-line approach in all situations, from making a purchase to attending a meeting, to how they function day-to-day in their job. They do not, however, like being told what to do. They seek practicality and alternatives, getting on with things as efficiently and quickly as possible in order to put one more issue or project behind them.

Can you keep this confidential? Many Golds, when they have errands to run, will write their to-do list in the order in which they plan to do them. Well, they wouldn't want to be inefficient, or waste time doubling back. And a lot of Golds, if they find they need to stop somewhere that wasn't on the list, will actually write it down, so they can cross it off right away!

Learning to Do Nothing and Enjoying It

Golds love accomplishing everything on their seemingly endless to-do lists. Until they've finished though, they're always in motion. Only when all their work is done will Golds give themselves permission to play and have fun, otherwise, just relaxing can seem irresponsible. After all, there are still things that need to be done: meals to prepare, rooms to be cleaned, paperwork to be organized, things to put away. Relaxing and having fun are things to be earned by completing a to-do list. *Don't worry, be happy?* Not likely, especially if there's one more thing to do ...

Doing nothing is almost impossible. Ask any Gold what they would do if they spotted a piece of lint on the living room sofa while watching television. Other Colors might not see anything, but Golds are usually hyper-aware of a piece of lint, a crooked picture or anything out of place. Would they ignore it, pick it up during the next commercial, or pick it up right away? Right away, of course, because Golds have a difficult time learning and embracing the simple art of doing nothing. They do try to relax and have fun, but it usually still involves some kind of task or planned activity – anything that is *something*, instead of *nothing*.

Relaxing can seem like hard work for Golds, because it doesn't accomplish anything and can seem a little irresponsible.

Planning the Work and Working the Plan

Golds are driven to do the right thing, the right way, on time, and according to plan. Preparation breeds confidence, the devil is in the details, and staying on task, on time, and efficient, is both incredibly satisfying and necessary for Golds to feel comfortable. Whether they are organizing a party or handling a project at work, Golds want to do it right; no details are too trivial and nothing must fall by the wayside. They will start a file, construct an outline, map out a timetable, gather their resources and work diligently until the task is completed.

It may seem like Golds never have fun, but that is not true at all. There is a time and a place for everything, and fun is for after work – right now they have a job to do. There are no points for effort, no credit given for an attempt – results are what matter. Golds give their word, they know others are relying on them, and they often feel as though the whole world is watching them. Golds are steady and consistent. They're happy to keep us from chaos and watch all the details.

First, they need a plan. After all, it would be quite irresponsible to just get going without a plan. A proper outline, detailed instructions and an organized agenda are valuable Gold tools. As children, they looked to evaluations and report cards to ensure they were doing a good job and completing assignments according to instructions. That was also when Golds first learned to ask detail-oriented questions: "Exactly how many pages does the book report need to be?" "Should it be double-spaced?" "When is it due?" "Does it count towards the grade?"

One of the Golds' many strengths lay in designing plans, systems, and procedures. Once a plan has been made and used successfully, it makes sense to keep the template for future use. *If it's not broken, don't fix it.* Plus, keeping the structure in place will speed up the process next time and allow Golds to increase their efficiency. To Golds, there is great safety and satisfaction in established routines and predictability.

Better Late Than Never? Better Never Late!

Planning and organizing necessitates staying on time, all the time. *If you're late, you're dead,* is the mentality. Being on time is not optional, and Golds are just as hard on themselves on this issue as they are intolerant of others. One of the biggest ways to honor and respect Golds is to be on time, every time. A 2 p.m. meeting means 2 p.m., not 2:10. Perceived or real, that ten-minute tardiness sends a clear message to Golds that the other person does not value or respect them.

> A *well-known, multi-national corporation in Vancouver, British Columbia, is owned by a very high Gold. Whether legend or fact, the story of how managers' meetings are conducted has been circulating for years. Apparently at the exact time these meetings are to start, the boardroom door is locked. Anyone late is simply unable to attend and then terminated from the company. Only once did a manager who arrived late actually take an axe from a nearby fire extinguisher box and break through the locked door. His ingenuity was rewarded by being allowed to attend the meeting — and to keep his job.*

The perception that others are wasting their time is a big stressor for Golds. Long lines, broken promises, excessive small talk, meetings with no agenda, inefficiencies, lack of organization, and changing decisions are all time-wasters that can drive Golds crazy.

A powerful way to delight Golds, professionally or personally, is to under-promise and over-deliver. Receiving a call that their order is ready early, or that their car is fixed ahead of schedule, is one of the most simple and powerful ways a business can retain this largest group of customers. Unfortunately, Golds know this rarely ever happens, so the next-best thing would be for a business or friend to be on time and to deliver as promised. The Gold mind-set demands no less; tardiness and excuses are not things Golds find easy to forgive.

Don't tell me when you THINK it MIGHT be done,
tell me specifically when it WILL be done,
and make sure that it is.

One Thing at a Time

Golds are very efficient. They are skilled time-management experts who work accurately and with single-minded focus towards deadlines and the completion of tasks. The vast majority of Golds work best when dealing with one thing at a time and prefer to complete one task before moving on to the next. This allows Golds to focus solely on the job at hand.

While they are dedicated and cooperative team players, Golds generally prefer to be responsible for one task from start to finish, assuring that the job will be done to their high standards and completed when promised. Imagine the Gold mind like a kitchen timer. When a task is begun, the timer starts. But there is only one timer, which runs until the task is completed. Only then will the timer restart and Golds are free to take on a new task. Golds will readily admit that having a number of projects on the go is a surefire way to increase their stress levels.

Golds measure their success – and how much fun they're having – by their accomplishments: when a task or a project is finished, and they can move on to the next thing on their to-do list. Multi-tasking is not a word Golds embrace. They usually believe that it is a recipe for disaster, disorganization, and trouble. Instead, they choose to stick to their agenda and plan, and with single-minded, step-by-step focus, see tasks through to completion.

Of course, like everyone else in today's society, sometimes Golds simply have to multi-task – and they certainly can. But they do have a strong belief that, in order to do things well, one thing should be completely done before moving on to the next. More often than not, Golds will scratch out an extra few minutes to completely finish and get something off their list and out of their mind. They often evade interruption, avoid answering the phone, ask someone to wait a few minutes, or just keep their head down and work, ignoring the world around them. To Golds, multi-tasking equals mediocre.

While that might seem harsh to other Colors, Golds see tremendous value in staying in control, and for them, things are simple: It's black or white, right or wrong perspective.

I want to start something. I want it done well,
and fully done, and THEN I want to move
on to the next thing.

Living In the Next Moment

Oranges live for right now; Golds live for right after that. Golds are always thinking ahead, looking to what has yet to be done, what could go wrong, and what needs to be finished, planned, or ordered. Golds are prepared and ready if – or when – something goes wrong, and there's always a plan B – a backup plan – just in case. It is not only the Scouts who must always be prepared – it's the Gold way of life.

Ask any Gold when they are most likely to start stressing about an important project: at 10 a.m. when they agree to take on the job, or closer to 4 p.m. when the job is due? Almost all will admit it is usually right after 10 a.m. when they start planning and worrying about ways to begin, what is involved, and how to make sure they will finish on time.

The Gold drive and focus on the *what ifs* is frequently misunderstood. But being Gold doesn't mean being negative. Golds' always hope for the best, they just like to anticipate potential pitfalls. And because what Golds plan usually turns out well, others often don't even notice the amount of effort they've put in to making sure that happens. Do other Colors appreciate all the Gold planning, thinking ahead, and preparation? Is it all worth it? You decide:

Red roses were her favorites, her name was also Rose. And every year her husband sent them, tied with pretty bows.

The year he died, the roses were delivered to her door. The card said "Be my valentine," like all the years before. Each year he sent her roses, and the note would always say, "I love you even more this year, than last year on this day. My love for you will always grow, with every passing year." She knew this was the last time that the roses would appear.

She thought, he ordered roses in advance before this day. Her loving husband did not know that he would pass away. He always liked to do things early, way before the time. Then, if he got too busy, everything would work out fine.

A year went by, and it was hard to live without her mate, with loneliness and solitude, that had become her fate. Then, the very hour, as on Valentines before, the doorbell rang, and there were roses, sitting by her door. She brought the roses in, and then just looked at them in shock. Then went to get the telephone to call the florist shop.

The owner answered, and she asked him if he would explain, why would someone do this to her, causing her such pain? "I know your husband passed away, more than a year ago," the owner said, "I knew you'd call, and you would want to know. The flowers you received today were paid for in advance. Your husband always planned ahead, he left nothing to chance. There is a standing order, that I have on file down here and he has paid, well in advance, you'll get them every year. There also is another thing that I think you should know. He wrote a special little card…he did this, years ago. Then, should ever I find out that he's no longer here that's the card that should be sent, to you the following year."

She thanked him and hung up the phone, her tears now flowing hard. Her fingers shaking as she slowly reached to get the card. Inside the card, she saw that he had written her a note. Then as she stared in total silence, this is what he wrote: "Hello my love, I know it's been a year since I've been gone. I hope it hasn't been too hard for you to overcome. I know it must be lonely, and the pain is very real. Or if it was the other way, I know how I would feel.

I know it's only been a year, but please try not to grieve. I want you to be happy, even when you shed your tears. That is why the roses will be sent to you for years. When you get these roses, think of all the happiness, that we had together and how both of us were blessed. I have always loved you and I know I always will. But my love, you must go on, you have

some living still. Please...try to find happiness, while living out
your days. I know it is not easy, but I hope you'll find some
ways. The roses will come every year, and they will only stop,
when your door's not answered when the florist stops to knock.

He will come five times that day, in case you have gone out.
But after his last visit, he will know without a doubt. To take
the roses to the place, where I've instructed him and place the
roses where we are – together once again."

James A. Kisner – adapted and used with permission

Tried, Tested, and True

Golds are creatures of habit who enjoy the safety and security of routines – the reason they stay loyal to their bank, dry cleaner, favorite coffee shop and grocery store. It is likely they have been customers for many years because of a combination of good service, promises kept, and value for money. Golds are quite fiscally conservative (some even say cheap). They certainly want a good deal, but they also know that sometimes the sweetness of a cheap price leads to the bitter taste of bad quality.

When Golds need to take their business elsewhere, they may feel sad and uncomfortable: sad because they can no longer rely on a trusted friend and uncomfortable because they now must shop around for an alternative and start a new relationship. Companies who understand the nature of Colors know that Golds are their most loyal customers and their greatest source of repeat business. Yet they must also understand and appreciate that with that loyalty come certain expectations. Golds will readily voice their displeasure over sub-standard customer service, broken promises, and price issues. Stonewalling, getting defensive, blaming, or ignoring Golds' feedback, is a surefire way to lose a ton of business very quickly.

When a company acknowledges a problem, apologizes, and makes amends, Golds become even more loyal customers. Things happen. But Golds offer customer feedback because they actually want to stay loyal.

Like most people, Golds have a favorite restaurant. It might take them a few minutes to name a second or third choice, but they have no trouble naming what they normally order. Why take a chance on something new? They'll order their usual because they know what to expect and their meal will taste great. Others may be impressed, thinking Golds are capable of quick decisions, but that is rarely the case: most have likely reached a decision before even getting to the restaurant. Glancing at the menu was just the polite thing to do.

The Gold need for stability and routine means other Colors must be aware of Golds' apprehension about changes to procedures or structures. Implementing significant changes may require patience and open communication over an extended period of time.

Golds prefer to have some options and input before buying in to any change. They value clear discussion, an outlining of the reasoning behind and benefits of any changes and a proposed timeline for those changes. Simply pushing changes through can become a significant stressor and may lead to backlash and resistance. It may not seem logical, but for Golds, there is safety in routines. Even good changes, like moving to a different place or a job promotion, will still be quite stressful.

A Special Gold Stress

Golds are strict rule followers. They believe that doing the right things and following all the rules means everything will go according to plan. This applies to their relationships and to raising their children, as well as to their work and career.

When Golds live their lives *by the book*, it creates a sense of safety and security. If they play by the rules, everything will turn out as planned. Four plus four always equals eight. Life, however, is nothing like a math equation. Golds still get divorced, are laid-off, and have bad things happen to them. When Golds have followed all the rules, and things still don't turn out the way they had anticipated, life can become extraordinarily difficult.

During stressful times, the Golds may start thinking that they need to work harder, do more, be more organized, or focus better. They may clean more, tidying everything. Thinking things will get back on track and life will turn around if they just do more is a common Gold reaction in times of trouble, hoping that their hard work, focus, and dedication will see them through bad situations. While that approach seldom works, since doing more is not the same as doing *better* or *different*, it is still a common Gold reaction.

> *Last Friday, you were really stressed about something. You are stressed every day, but what was it last Friday? Of course you don't remember. Keep that in mind the next time (today) when you allow something small, trivial, or external to have that much power and influence over you. Take a few seconds to put it into perspective: Will this still matter tomorrow, next week, or next year?*

First, We Clean Up

Before they start work, and even before relaxing at home, Golds first need to clean up. They usually can't focus or concentrate unless they have taken a few minutes to get organized. From their desks to their closets, their garages to their kitchen counters, Golds are anti-mess.

At a dinner party, as soon as the dessert is finished, Golds will probably start to clear the table and load the dishwasher. They are not trying to signal that it's time for the get-together to be over, but are simply cleaning up so that they can relax and enjoy the rest of their evening. Even when Golds hire a cleaning person, they most likely do some of the cleaning in advance. ("I wouldn't want anyone to think I'm messy.")

Golds love Ikea and The Container Store. At home, there is definitely a place for everything and everything in its place, and few things are more satisfying. Other Colors may not notice or care, but for Golds, it is very calming and relaxing to have their world neat and tidy.

At work, Golds have this same mind-set. Whether it's a desk or a workbench, tools are in their proper place and paperwork is neatly organized. For Golds, being neat, clean, tidy, and organized creates a strong sense of calmness and control over their work and their world. But can this be taken too far? At Audi's headquarters in Herdon, Virginia, corporate policy actually mandates that every employee's desk must be paper-free at the end of the day. Not a problem for Golds, who make up the largest group of managers, but a big problem for all the other Colors. Other companies whose culture is also very much Gold-influenced, including General Electric and UPS, have similar policies, but theirs take the form of goals rather than company-wide mandates.

Don't Touch My Stuff

From the clothes they buy to the cars they drive, Golds take pride in their possessions. They prefer expensive, quality items that will last a long time, maintaining and keeping their cars and clothes for years rather than replacing them.

The Gold pride of ownership causes conflict when others ask to borrow things. While Golds have a hard time saying no, they are also reluctant to lend most anything to anybody, even down to something as inconsequential as their office supplies. Golds take very good care of their possessions and believe that many other people … don't. Plus, Golds get frustrated when something is not returned promptly (even though they have a hard time telling the borrower so).

If Golds need something, they almost always buy it for themselves rather than borrowing. If and when Golds ever do need to borrow something, returning it is priority number one. They believe it is a serious responsibility to be entrusted with someone else's possessions. (They wish everyone shared that value.) And when Golds return the item, it is in the same condition (or better, or cleaner, or neater) as they received it.

What You See and Hear from Golds

Golds tend to wear traditional and conservative attire and are more reserved in demeanor. They are generally private and controlled, polite but not effusive. Remember that Golds value a bottom-line approach, which will likely come across in their tone. Golds can also often be identified by their Blackberries or extensive personal organizers.

They prefer an organized workspace and a neat and tidy home. Often there are bulletin boards and lots of lists, memo pads, and sticky notes. Golds value functionality and practicality – and definitely not clutter. Golds also like to have clocks in plain view, and they frequently look at their watches. Knowing what time it is, is their compass for the day.

Golds maintain an even and business-like tone in their conversations and often word things in an either-or, black-or-white manner. They ask for specifics and details and are not interested in generalities. All of this can make Golds appear impatient. They tolerate just enough small talk to be polite before getting to the point. They want to know the rules, the structure, and the chain of command, and they prefer to talk about one subject at a time before moving on.

With a preference for short and to-the-point conversations, Golds tend to speak in lists: "First we should ..." and it is why they ask mostly yes-or-no questions. The Gold goal is to finish things – even if it's just a conversation.

Now I Understand...

Your strength is in getting it done. But not just done – done right, done now, and always when promised. In the same way, you do things because they need doing – unquestioningly, unwaveringly, and consistently.

I understand how you distinguish between a home and a house, a job and a career, and doing something right versus just doing something. Those are some of the special ways that set you apart from others.

You look to be acknowledged for your efforts. So often, your work and your help are over and above what anyone could ask for. "Like a Rock" really does describe you.

Planning and doing things in good order creates a sense of stability and safety in your future and for those around you.

You are a private person and don't allow everyone into your life. I feel special and honored because you are a true friend, not just a buddy.

You really can't say no very often. Your strong sense of duty always shows when you help others and when you give back to your community in many special ways.

No one is harder on themselves than you are – most often needlessly. When it is in moderation, it is the drive that keeps you on-task and focused.

You don't live in the past but keep many special traditions and values alive that provide an invaluable link to the future.

I am your boss or your friend. I am your partner, someone you work with, or your relative … and now I understand you a little better.

Common Gold Strengths

Accurate and detail-oriented
Clear expectations
Conscientious
Considerate and empathetic
Conventional
Direct and efficient
Valuing family and friends
Giving and helpful
Loyal
Practical
Punctual
Self-motivated
Thorough
Strong-willed
Open to criticism

Cautious and traditional
Confident
Committed
Consistent and dependable
Decisive and in control
Fair and honest
Focused
Frugal
Organized
Predictable
Responsible and reliable
Self-confident
Stable and structured
Supportive
Willing to take charge

Common Gold Stressors

Action before planning
Being taken advantage of
Clutter and disorganization
Bottled up emotions
Exceptions to rules
Getting sidetracked
Having to rely on others
Inefficiency and long lines
Lack of clear instructions
Disloyalty or lack of respect
Not having enough time – ever
Indecisiveness in others
People who don't follow through
Too much responsibility

Tardiness
Change in routine
Unpredictability
Equipment that doesn't work
Feeling overworked
Having to say no
Being responsible for others
Interruptions
Last-minute changes
Non-productive meetings/work
Loss of control
Worrying too much
Taking on too much
Too many things unfinished

Yeah, feels weird. This is our first night at home in 2 weeks. It's not right... we've got to do something tonight...

That was a gift from work, since I'm the Queen of handling challenges and putting out fires.

Chapter Four

Oranges: Freedom and Skillfulness

The drive to enjoy life to the fullest and to multi-task.

The focus of: "Just Do It" and "Let's Go!"

Prefer to enjoy the spontaneity of the moment.

A classic line: *"Winning isn't everything – it's the only thing!"*

A great quote: *"Hey, I'm just someone who can make quick decisions and think on my feet. I'm sorry you can't."*
Talk show host Charles Adler

I believe that life is a game filled with fun, variety and creativity, and it should be played to win. I love competition and interaction, but not too much planning or structure. I avoid boredom and routine at almost all costs. I am a natural troubleshooter, who doesn't mind rolling up my sleeves and getting involved. I greatly value my freedom, and I'm known for my courage and my high energy level. I'm ready and able to act on a moment's notice – just watch me!

When an Orange comes into our life, we know it. They are easy to spot by their enthusiastic attitude, sense of humor and playful nature. Oranges enjoy being noticed and recognized, and they have no problem with being the center of attention. They enjoy being different and love to show off – both themselves and their latest, greatest, and coolest stuff. From the clothes they wear to the cars they drive, image is very important. They act, talk, and dress like winners.

Get To the Point

Oranges have a unique communication style which is sometimes a challenge for other Colors to understand. They love rapid, back-and-forth exchanges and look for immediate results and feedback. In other words, call them, text them, or catch them, instead of using mail, fax, or e-mail. They want quick answers and decisions, and any delay can bring out their impatient streak.

Oranges are not above cutting someone off when an answer or explanation starts to drag. They don't want that much information, nor do they need to make up their minds. If you can't explain something in the length of time it takes to ride an escalator, then you shouldn't even bother. While this bottom-line approach may seem rude, it is not intended to be. Oranges simply want people to get to the point, keep it positive, make it quick, and tell it like it is – now.

Every Orange does experience the occasional "Orange moment," when they wish they could take their words back. Oranges' shoot-from-the-hip style can sometimes be difficult to take, and speaking without thinking can get them into trouble. When this happens, they do feel bad, but not too bad, and certainly not for long. They believe you shouldn't ask a question if you don't want to hear the answer.

A Different Kind of Creativity

Oranges, along with their Blue friends, are very creative. They develop ideas and plans by talking things through, working out and perfecting the details as they go along. You can actually hear as they start to talk before they've thought anything through: "If we want to really promote that, we could get someone to – no, that won't work. What if we all get up and ... No, I've got it! We should ..." Should others interrupt or cut them off, they may very well miss the fourth or fifth idea, which was likely to have been the perfect solution and something few others would have thought of.

Because of their creativity, large numbers of Oranges are drawn to the fields of construction, design and renovation, along with a wide range of other "hands-on" professions. Where others might simply see the blueprint, Oranges can imagine the finished project down to the smallest details. An abandoned, run-down, old house with shag carpeting and dingy windows easily becomes a dream house, as Oranges visualize and the home's incredible potential is realized: "We need to tear down this wall, change these windows, dark hardwood floor, light chocolate paint throughout, double the size of the kitchen, take out this bedroom and convert it to a huge walk-in closet …" Excited and impatient to get started, Oranges have a vision, and the doubters will just have to get out of the way!

In addition to the many house or room makeover shows, there are also a few which specialize in restaurants. One particularly insightful episode featured an Orange designer and her vision against two Green restaurant partners. During the first quarter of the show, the designer attempted to convince both owners that their place was dingy and dark, full of ancient decor, crappy clutter, and a bar that looked like it was built by a child. It became apparent that she wanted to (make that: was going to) gut the place, whereas the owners had been looking for a new paint job at most.

When it comes to creativity and visualizing the renovation process, or envisioning decorating changes, always bet on the Orange and trust them on this! The same holds true for most high Blues. This Orange was not going to cave in, settle, compromise, or make a deal of any kind. She was also the reason this episode had a coarse language warning — not something that would be necessary with a Blue designer.

What was her solution to the impasse? Agree to the owners' minor changes and just get them to leave. But then, the typical Orange mindset tends to be: I'd rather ask for forgiveness than permission, or: Yea – whatever – I'm going to do this and you'll love it when I'm done! (Yes – news flash: they do that at work, too!)

Within a couple of hours, her crew had gutted the entire restaurant. But imagine the look of horror on the face of the owners! Having reached the point of no turning back, the designer commented that they might as well keep going now, which simply had the hyperventilating owners leave again. While, at the start, she may have had no credibility with the Green owners, the end result was worth it when the comments started with "nice and good" but quickly escalated to "awesome and amazing."

Need to plan a Christmas party, come up with new ideas with your team, or hold a church fundraiser? It makes a big difference when an Orange is involved. These are areas where our Orange friends and teammates excel. For them, it's fun, not work, and they love a challenge. They will produce extraordinary results, but in the words of a bumper sticker, everyone else better, "*Sit down, hold on, and shut up.*"

Nothing is Set in Stone

Oranges are incredibly flexible, and they don't get hung up on routines since everything is open to negotiation and change is good. The ability to think on their feet and a healthy appreciation for competition are two attributes which contribute to making many

Oranges such powerful and successful salespeople. Oranges almost always hear *no* as *maybe*, and use their charm, humor, and persuasiveness to turn it into *yes*. That's assuming they even stop to hear the word *no*. Usually it's full speed ahead, pursuing the sale and finding a way to get what they want. Maybe all that's needed is a new approach or a different angle. From the time they were children, Oranges have used their verbal skills to talk their way into or out of things – and they've been fine-tuning these skills ever since.

Yes We Can

Almost all Oranges have tremendous self-confidence. They know that their attitude controls their altitude – and their quality of life. Their eternal optimism is not phony or practiced, but an ever-present part of their nature – the DNA of their Color. Even in difficult times, Oranges will stay positive and unwavering, believing that the next day, the next project, or the next client, will always be better. Until then, Oranges will fake it until they make it.

The Orange winning attitude combined with the drive to succeed creates a powerful combination. Throw in commission, recognition, or a dare, and Oranges are well on their way to becoming seriously motivated.

> *Passion on fire is way better than knowledge on ice.*
> Shane Rudman

Show Me the Money

Money is a double-edged sword for Oranges. They likely earn a good salary, and they are very generous, but there never seems to be enough of it. While almost everyone could say "there never seems to be enough," for Oranges, it's a serious issue.

Oranges tend to make a lot of money and then spend it just as quickly. It is rare for Oranges to be concerned with price, instead thinking "if it's worth having, it's worth buying." Oranges are impulsive decision-makers. No self-respecting Orange will spend hours at the mall. *Get in, get it, and get out! Find it, like it, buy it – the end.* Money is for gadgets and fun and cool stuff, and whoever has the most toys wins. And by the way, winning is everything!

No wonder Oranges are motivated by commission-based pay and bonus plans. These types of compensation plans offer Oranges the freedom to do whatever it takes to control the size of their own paycheck, so when they run short of money, they have the ability to earn more. Bonus plans, tips, and commissions are concrete motivators which allow Oranges to live the lifestyle they choose – and to be rewarded in direct proportion to their talents and efforts.

Oranges are very generous with their friends and family. Forget dividing the check. Why waste time on something so silly? "Here's some money – let's get out of here," makes much more sense.

Releasing Some Energy

The two most common New Year's resolutions are the resolution to work out more and the resolution to become better organized. The first one is hardly ever made by Oranges. Most have long ago realized that being physically active is important for releasing all their pent-up energy. That energy is easy to see. Right now, your Orange co-worker is probably playing with a pen, tapping their feet, shuffling in their chair, getting up, or doodling.

After just a week of no physical activity, most Oranges will admit to feeling fidgety, a little stir-crazy, and ready to explode. Thank goodness Oranges are the most faithful and active members of fitness clubs. They may enjoy walking, running, mountain biking, softball, or other team sports.

The second resolution, that of becoming better organized, is a challenge for Oranges. While organization is in the eye of the beholder, and they will never buy into the Gold definition of neat piles and labeled boxes, for Oranges, being organized means being able to find what they need, when they need it. It's a real challenge. And while most Oranges wish they were more organized, it is not enough of a priority for them to make it happen to any significant degree, anytime soon. They may as well add that to next year's resolution list now.

Winging It

Oranges are incredible multi-taskers who love to have many things on the go and can juggle a ton of projects with ease. Staying crazy-busy is an adrenalin rush and makes life much more fun. Oranges do not worry about some due date down the road. It's the *right now* deadlines which cause them to scramble, get focused, and get it done. Having lunch and suddenly remember a report that is due in an hour? No problem! It will all work out, and there's no reason to panic. Too much preparation is highly over-rated and totally unnecessary. Ulcers are something Oranges might cause, but they are the least likely Color to suffer from them.

Oranges prefer to wing it, keep their options open, and see what happens. They function best when they can think on their feet and figure everything out as they go along. They don't want to waste time and energy on needless preparation. It makes much more sense to stay flexible, be open to better ideas, and adapt to change as it comes. Changing priorities is never a problem.

Most other Colors share these Orange traits as children, but Oranges are fortunate to retain these strengths throughout adulthood. Not too much planning, thinking on their feet, less worry and more fun – it's the Orange way and it's something to cherish.

Just Do It!

Oranges can be successful at anything they set their minds to, but that success comes from hands-on effort, rather than from reading theory, textbooks, or manuals. They need to *do it*, instead of talking or reading about it. Oranges want to know what time it is, not how the watch was made. A long, detailed explanation will have them showing their impatience. When that happens, they are not above cutting someone off and asking for the bottom line.

Recently, an Orange friend called me in total frustration. She needed a new heating and A/C system. A salesperson came to her house, and she told him that she was not an expert, her system had conked out, and she wanted a new one installed. Well, not so fast. The salesperson was a very high Green, and the Colors conflict soon started. The questions were endless as to what she needed, wanted, might consider, and so on.

With every question my Orange friend became more impatient. She kept telling the salesperson that she just wanted the system replaced, she trusted him, she didn't know the specs, but that he could recommend what he felt was appropriate and it'd be a done deal. Nope – it wasn't that simple. It turned into another ten minutes of explaining various options, features, advantages, drawbacks, and more.

By now, my friend's head was ready to explode, and she turned her efforts toward doing whatever she could to get the salesperson out of her house. To her, the whole thing was like quicksand, and she was stuck. She answered phone calls, tried to explain she really had to go, and even started her car! When the sales person finally did leave, her first call was to me. "I just wanted to buy the system. I just wanted to write a check and be done with it. But he wouldn't let me!"

My friend had no interest in the inner workings of a heating system. She just wanted to get it replaced! Communicating, like selling, is not about you. It's about the person you are dealing with. We can over-talk, over-explain and over-sell. Be careful, and watch the many clues Oranges give to "hurry it up." Or in this case, watch the waving check book, shut up, and get the order!

Oranges believe that the best way to do something is to do it, not sit around talking about it. They jump first, and build their wings on the way down. They figure things out as they go along, knowing that for them, real-life situations, where the adrenaline is pumping and there is something at stake, will produce the greatest results. Oranges believe extensive preparation, having to read the manual, or engaging in long-winded strategy discussions are all highly overrated. Or as Sir Richard Branson describes his business philosophy in his book, *Losing My Virginity*, "Oh, screw it, let's do it."

It's no wonder most Oranges choose to work in action-oriented, hands-on fields, ranging from police and firefighters to customer service, sales and marketing to electricians and plumbers. But the dream job for many Oranges is professional athlete or media star. Oranges are natural performers, and even though the odds of making it as a baseball player or talk show host are stacked against them, that just makes it all the more fun to climb to the top, and all the sweeter when they get there. Oranges are certainly well able to deal with constant change, the high-risk of failure, and the almost-permanent need to think on their feet and adapt to new situations. Oranges are very rarely self-conscious, or worry about what others might think.

These traits serve Oranges well in the music business, where many well-known Orange musicians push boundaries, experiment, and try the impossible, without being held back by rules. That is real freedom; it is the Orange definition of truly living, and not just in the music industry.

Oranges want to be judged on results, not attempts, because they're all about experimenting. Results are always the goal. Whether an actor winning the Oscar, a salesperson landing the big contract after months of negative feedback, the band starting their first world tour, or a child starring in the class play, victories and successes are the tangible goals Oranges have been striving for.

Ultimately, Oranges are very successful in careers which interest them, hold their attention, and offer the opportunity to "win." Until they find their place and reach that point, it's important that others not "force" Oranges. Parents, co-workers, friends, and bosses often place emphasis on the process, rather than the results. Being supportive of Orange dreams and seemingly impossible goals is challenging, but much better than judging them based on the values of the other Colors.

The Drive to Win

From sporting events to sales contests or board games, Oranges want to win. This drive is a large part of their identity. Whoever coined the saying, *it's not whether you win or lose, its how you play the game*, wasn't an Orange. It is no wonder vast numbers of them become professional athletes.

Nothing is sweeter than the taste of victory. Oranges can,
and almost always do, make most things into a contest.
It not only helps them to focus, but it also acts as
a huge motivator and provides a great adrenalin rush.

Down by two touchdowns, behind by six runs, eight strokes back, or currently seventh in the sales contest: It's time for an Orange to get serious. Others might be ready to give up, but Oranges are just getting motivated. Having their back against the wall is a wakeup call. When the pressure is on, the rest of the world has given up, and nobody believes that they can pull it off or come out on top, that's fun! It's what makes victory so sweet. The competition, the drive to win, other like-minded people who won't back down from a challenge, all that media attention, all those fans … yes!

The money is great too, but that's not the primary motivator. More than one professional athlete has said publicly that he'd play the game for free; it's the practices he needs to be paid for. Out there on the field – or even in the office – when everyone is counting on them, that's where real life happens! Nike's *Just do it* slogan is also the Orange motto. (Plus, it's no coincidence that Nike is the name of the Greek goddess of Victory.)

Winning makes Oranges winners. And maybe practice does make
perfect. But if being a gracious loser takes practice, Oranges will
never be good at it. They just refuse to lose enough!

Oranges know that nobody remembers who came in second. Second is just the first loser, as far as they're concerned, so when it comes to winning, Oranges very much share their Gold friends' black-or-white mind-set. If they believe they cannot be successful, Oranges often choose not to participate in the first place. But once they are committed to a game, a contest, or a project, Oranges will be all business – no sight-seeing, no distractions, no detours, no excuses. Their friendships will endure, but they might have to take a backseat for the time being.

The drive to win can also show itself during discussions or arguments. Oranges do not fight fair – they fight to win. They may bring up something that happened years ago, dodge or avoid an issue, or lash out verbally. One of their favorite ways to end an argument is, "Whatever!" When this happens, it is best for the other person to understand that they have made their point and to let it go. Prolonging the argument will only make things worse.

A Special Orange Challenge

For years, many Oranges have been labeled as rule-breakers and troublemakers. Most of the structure created by our Gold society can not contain Oranges' style and personality. Oranges typically challenge rules and question boundaries. They do have strong value systems, but they are uniquely theirs. Some Oranges were never taught to, and some are not interested in, conforming to what the world considers appropriate behaviors.

On the other side of the coin, there are huge numbers of extremely successful Oranges – managers, CEOs, and most entrepreneurs. These Oranges, who conform to the basic rules and norms of society, have not given up their fight for freedom or uniqueness, but rather have channeled their energies, talents, and drive to win in a positive direction. They are often unstoppable.

I will not be how you want me to be … I will be how I choose to be!

T.G.

Hurry Up

From cars to conversations, Oranges love speed and action. Other Colors might have a hard time keeping up, but Oranges are not about to slow down. Their never-ending search for adventure means energy and optimism are constants.

Even decisions come quickly. Oranges do not have the time to linger, so conversations and discussions may quickly jump from one topic to another. Other Colors need to be flexible – an Orange conversation can keep you on your toes. If an Orange calls with an invitation to do something, they are likely already in their car and on their way to pick you up. Seldom will anyone have much notice or time to decide whether or not they want to come along. If it takes too long to decide, well, no problem, Oranges are happy to go without you. Your loss.

"I was retired for 12 hours. Eight of those I slept, and then I wanted to start a new business."

Buddy – owner of Finn McCool Restaurant

Salespeople who are unable to speed up, or to switch gears when targeting presentations to Orange customers, will see Oranges leaving the store empty-handed. In fact, studies have shown that more than $20 billion in merchandise is left at checkout counters each year by frustrated customers. It would not be much of a stretch to assume the majority of these lost customers are Oranges, who refuse to waste time standing in long lines. What a waste!

ADD? Not Likely

Attention Deficit Disorder (ADD) is something plenty of Oranges have been asked about or labeled with. In fact, drug makers now claim that over eight million adults in North America suffer from ADD. Maybe. Without downplaying the legitimacy of ADD, there are many Oranges who laugh at the diagnosis and know full well that many of their "symptoms" are normal behaviors – for an Orange.

The web site of one drug maker claims that a simple six-question quiz establishes whether or not someone is likely to be diagnosed with ADD. The assessment questions consider whether the person has trouble finishing projects, has difficulty sitting still for long periods without fidgeting, experiences challenges getting started on detailed projects, or has trouble planning tasks in order. There are very few Oranges who would not answer yes to all of those questions – otherwise, they wouldn't be Orange!

Are these really symptoms, or just special gifts and talents? A project can always be finished at the last minute. Right now, Oranges have lots of others things on their plates. Sitting still is not always a challenge, but it does depend on whether a meeting or project is interesting and interactive, and makes sense. Planning tasks and putting them in order is not half as much fun as working on pieces here and there, a little bit at a time. It all creates variety while avoiding boredom – it does not necessarily create a need for drugs. Oranges will get their work done, and while it may not be done using the same template and method as the rest of the world, it is going to be a lot more fun along the way.

Oranges have the ability to multi-task with ease, and with little or no stress. They have the drive to be challenged. Even if that means they may also be impulsive, easily distracted, and have a tendency to avoid paperwork, it's still a pretty good trade-off.

Thank heavens for my understanding Colors, or I would have been making a huge mistake with my Orange daughter. She does drive me crazy with ten things on the go. But, instead of yelling at her, and making things worse, I have learned unbelievable patience and gentle nudging. Believe it or not, it works! It is hard to resist the urge to become judgmental, jump in, or hurry her along. But an understanding of how Oranges think and act helps our family, strengthens our relationship, and will equip her for a lifetime of success and not medication.

C.G.

Many critics are even harsher, describing much of the two-billion-dollar ADD drug industry as marketing lifestyle drugs. While the truth is likely somewhere in the middle, the tools and insights of Colors certainly play a large role in understanding Oranges and their great strengths, skills, and unique outlook on life.

Friends and Buddies

Oranges love to be around other people. They are approachable and friendly, and their easygoing attitude, great sense of humor and extremely social nature often makes them the life of the party. Oranges have a gift for making anyone and everyone feel like they are important. They have a large circle of friends and an incredible array of contacts. If someone needs to connect with a business, get a referral, find a new employee, or track down a great new restaurant, Oranges are the go-to people. They will know somebody, or they will know somebody who knows somebody …

The Heck with What They Think

Without the insights of Colors, many people wonder about their Orange friends, family members, or co-workers. When will they grow up, act more responsibly, be more serious, get better organized, or shape up? The answer is, never. A strong independent streak, the drive to perform, and the need to be the star, mean Oranges have no interest in what others may think of them. Their self-confidence is not based on the opinions of others, and they wouldn't be half as successful as they are if they cared about conforming, fitting in, or being politically correct. What you see is what you get, and what you get is exactly who they are.

It was actually her grandson who brought Karen to the seminar. It was just after her 75th birthday, and somehow her grandson had enough insight to know that she would get lots of value from understanding Colors.

For the first part, she sat quietly, smiled a lot, and just listened. But when the Color groups were separated, Karen quickly joined the Oranges. She was and is a high Orange! The last ten years in a nursing home hadn't changed her at all but had certainly created a mask. A mask that was perhaps meant to hide who she really was, but after all those years had actually started to define her instead.

Age had not changed Karen's personality. It had simply mellowed her, reduced her volume control, and her physical energy was certainly a lot less in comparison to a 20-something Orange. But she still bugged people all the time to play cribbage, cards, or some kind of game where she could have some competition and the chance to win. She was friends with everyone in the nursing home and the staff loved her.

At the end of the seminar she shared with me: "I'm back! And I'm gonna buy a canoe! I've always wanted to have a canoe to be out on the lake and to have freedom to go wherever I want and whenever I want. I'm going to do it!"

I don't know if Karen ever did buy that canoe. It was never about the canoe anyway, but about seeing the sparkle in her eyes that morning and about an Orange person finding the words and explanations to understand who she really is. Perhaps it was giving herself permission to be who she really was and is, and to put away the mask of conformity.

What You See and Hear from Oranges

It is always easy to spot a high Orange. They like to dress in the latest styles. They seem to always have the newest, coolest gadgets. Their workspace can be quite messy, and they may have some sports equipment lying around. If they have pictures on the wall, these may include some of themselves with famous people, or receiving an award, or attending a well-known sporting event. They tend to misplace things. Oranges have an active and confident demeanor. Sitting still for extended periods of time is a real challenge. They don't hide their impatience.

When you listen to an Orange, you can sense the high energy level. Even in church, it is usually easy to tell when a group of Oranges have arrived. They love laughter and humor. In conversation, they quickly jump from subject to subject, talking quite fast in an animated voice. They are natural name-droppers, using it to connect with others. After all, if we both know so-and-so, we are practically friends already! Oranges are constantly networking, promoting ideas and businesses. They often ask probing and direct questions. They want to discuss the big picture without getting bogged down by details. Other Colors must know to keep conversations to the point, stay flexible, and bring their sense of humor.

Now I Understand...

I recognize that being on time is often a challenge and may be more important to me than to you. The clock does not measure the value of our relationship.

I value and look for your high energy, which makes you a magnet for others who seek you out. I can't duplicate it, but I also gain energy from being around you.

Sometimes my role is to finish up something, or to pick up the pieces. Yes, I may grumble or complain, but I also know that if it weren't for you, we probably wouldn't have gotten started at all.

You teach me not to be too serious. I continue to learn that it is okay to laugh at myself. You pull me out of my shell. Sometimes I fight or resist – but you don't give up.

You teach in ways others don't – not through textbooks or talking. You do it by example, by rolling up your sleeves and actually doing.

Your ability to change tacks and your "let's go" attitude is something I value learning from you. Sometimes I may not participate, but I always love watching you in action. With you there is seldom a dull moment.

Few others have your combination of talent and personality. You value freedom as much as others value knowing you. I was a lot more like you as a kid. Watching you, I sometimes wonder how the world has closed in on me, while you have managed to keep so much of your free spirit.

I am your boss or your friend. I am your partner, someone you work with or your relative ... and now I understand you a little better.

Common Orange Strengths

Active

Artistic

Direct

Energetic

Spontaneous

Unpredictable

Sense of humor

Sense of fun

Impulsive

Exciting

Skillful

Open-minded

Outrageous and vocal

Ready and able to change

Social

Adventurous

Successful at sales

Taking things in stride

Entertaining

Flexible

Generous

Handy

Impatient

Just do it! attitude

Attention seeking

Loyal and caring

Optimistic

People magnet

Risk-taker

Common Orange Stressors

Boredom and lack of action

Slow people

Fixed rules and policies

Having to be on time

Lack of choices

Making lists

Meetings and deadlines

Non-party people

Lack of recognition

Whiners, complainers and worriers

Rigid schedules

Sappy songs

Paperwork

Conformity

Losing

Sore losers

Losing things

Manuals and procedures

Needy people

Lack of challenges

Shortage of funds

Political correctness

Routines

Sitting still

No, when they said you had a "Green face"
they weren't talking about anything medical.

I agree we want the perfect computer system.
But it's our first anniversary, we should really get it soon...

Chapter Five

Greens: Knowledge and Understanding

The desire to gather the facts and research all of the options
before making a decision.

The focus on a lifetime of learning and exploring.

Examining all of life's experiences,
searching for the potential for improvement.

A classic line: *Sarcasm is humor too.*

A great quote: *Either find a way, or make one yourself.*

*I believe in remaining calm, cool, and collected in any
situation. I value knowledge and learning and enjoy passing
that knowledge on to others who want to learn. I am intelligent
and logical and can be a perfectionist. I am analytical and
enjoy thinking things through. I want to explore all possibilities
and avenues in my creative and inventive way before
committing myself or making a decision. I prefer to look at the
big picture and can consistently be counted on to provide
accurate and logical information and answers.*

Greens live in a world of facts and logic, quite different from Blues
who function through intuition and feelings. Greens are leaders. They
have sharp minds and a never-ending desire to grow – questioning the
status quo and pursuing a lifetime of learning. Consequently, Greens are
often steps ahead of others in terms of their plans, ideas, and visions.

Greens greatly value knowledge and understanding. They thrive on constant mental challenges, and they've never met a problem they didn't want to tackle. They believe curiosity takes courage. Greens both exhibit and look for logic and competence, not only in their thought processes, but in the people they work with, and in the framework or structure of their environments. They are the trendsetters and the visionaries, never the "yes" people or the followers. Conforming to the norm is of little interest to Greens. They were strong-willed and independent as children, and continue to be so as adults.

Information is Power

Greens love to learn. It is a life-long pursuit – a desire for knowledge that serves them well. This continual search for understanding means the Green mind is constantly processing and analyzing everything they encounter. For them, information truly is power.

> *"Strange how much you've got to know*
> *before you know how little you know."*
> Author Unknown

Questioning how something works, and why certain procedures are in place, or searching for and finding improved tools, technology, and processes are Green special strengths. They focus on the big picture and enjoy solving complex problems. They may become annoyed and frustrated when they are unable to access credible information, or when current procedures or methods are no longer efficient or even logical. Greens cannot conceive how anyone would settle for sub-par when there are clearly better ways of doing things.

Greens might not give in, but they
sure would not give up, either.

Greens are constantly thinking. Even in the checkout line, they're evaluating and examining the store's inefficiencies and wondering what might work better. The downside is that there is no "off" switch. Most Greens admit that there are nights when it can take hours to fall asleep, simply because they cannot turn off their thought processes.

Greens are driven to learn and grow, and they look for complete and accurate information – answers to their "why?" and "how?" questions. So, imagine their motivation when it comes to their own life and death decision:

The Patient from Hell is the title of a book by Professor Stephen Schneider. It's also how some old-school medical professionals might describe their Green patients. Should they become seriously ill, Greens want to, and need to, learn as much as they can about their illness. They want to understand every option and decision that will be involved in their treatment.

For Stephen Schneider, this included a lot of internet research, despite being told by his doctor that such searches would both depress and confuse him. Wrong! Schneider believes his persistence and willingness played a key role in his being alive today. From talking a surgeon out of his scheduled biopsy surgery, to the simple use of a needle, to changes in medication, he challenged specialists and unearthed information critical for his treatment. Schneider is now in remission, something he fully credits to taking charge of his own destiny.

Dealing with Hurt Feelings

When Greens are hurt, they care and feel just as deeply as every other Color, but when they are hurting, Greens prefer to be alone. They are not comfortable sharing their feelings with other people, nor is their hurt or sadness easily apparent. They unplug the telephone, tune out the world, and turn on (or turn to) their computer.

It is uncomfortable, and very unusual, for Greens to show their feelings in public. They do not believe they will somehow feel better by talking about it. If Greens do discuss their feelings or frustrations, it will likely be with another Green, who will ensure that the conversation stays logical and rational. As the earlier story of Stephen Schneider illustrates, for Greens, there is nothing that can't be solved by the combination of research, information, and alone time.

Emotional outbursts and public displays of affection, are quite rare with Greens. They can offer verbal affirmations for their staff, or hold hands with their partner in public, but these things are out of a Green's comfort zone. Yes, someone is doing a good job, and they certainly do love their partner, but it is not something that needs to be said or shown all the time.

Mother's Day Facebook post: *My Mother's Day was the same as any other. That's the norm for Mother's Day, our anniversary, Christmas, and my birthday. I have to celebrate on my own.*

Next day note: *Just wanted to clarify my note from yesterday. I wanted to add that I love my husband, and he loves me, but gift-giver and celebrator he is not. I have learned to value that he shows me love in other ways.*

A.K.P.

Bluff Me and I'm Gone

Greens value credibility above most things. Any business, salesperson, or co-worker who bluffs their way through a question or lies to a Green, is finished. (Most Greens will admit that this includes family and friends as well – no special exemptions granted!) It is perfectly OK though, to tell a Green that you do not have the answer. Just get back to them with the information – preferably by e-mail, with correct spelling and grammar – when promised.

Trial lawyers believe that one should never ask a question without knowing the answer. Greens often practice this approach as well. In a meeting, at a store, or with a staff member, they often ask one or two questions to which they already know the answers. Why? Simply to test the credibility of the other person.

Green Time

The generally accepted definition of organization is the Gold definition: neat piles, a clean desk, and labeled file folders. Yet the word *organization*, like the definitions of *family*, *honesty*, and *fun*, has a very different definition for each Color. If Greens are asked what being organized means – either the Gold definition, or having one's thoughts organized – almost all will describe being mentally organized.

This is why every Green needs to have a certain amount of alone time – Green time – each day. They need to think things through, process information, figure something out, plan their strategies, or work through a problem.

While others, including their different-Colored partners, can misinterpret this as antisocial behavior, or think that perhaps they're angry, nothing could be further from the truth. This independent processing and thinking time is simply necessary – both invaluable and mandatory. It might manifest as working on a project in the garage, going for a walk, spending some time on the computer, or reading. Green time is when Greens may unwind and reflect.

At parties and social functions, Greens generally start to drift to the sidelines after an hour or two. They enjoy these occasions as much as anyone, but only for limited periods of time. Then their energy levels start to drain, and they prefer not to be in the middle of the action and noise, but are quite content to people-watch from the sidelines. Besides, they may meet another Green doing the same thing and be able to strike up a great conversation.

Recently, our family hosted the current reigning World Junior Champions in their sport for a tournament against the Chinese National Team, here to train for the Olympics.

After breakfast, Chris, the captain, got up from the table and sat outside in his car, all alone, without a word to anyone. As I sat staring out the window at him wondering what was wrong, one of the other boys came up to me and said, "Don't take it personally. Chris just gets moody. We've learned to just ignore him when he's like that." And after about 20 minutes sitting in the car, Chris drove off alone, leaving the rest of the team to pack up all the equipment and arrange their own transportation.

Later that evening, they spotted the Colorful Personalities book. Chris immediately took the quiz, and as he read the characteristics of Greens he had just a hint of a grin. And this is most unusual for Chris, as they call him "poker face" because his face remains the same, whether his dog just died, or he's won the lottery. When his teammates did the assessment, he bluntly challenged one of them for not being honest. It was something his teammate admitted, as he was afraid the others would think he was too soft. To which Chris replied, "But every team needs a Blue!" He couldn't have paid his teammate a higher compliment!

The next morning, Chris again snuck off to the car for his alone time, but his team now laughed and commented, "That's our Green Chris." But today it was said with pride, respect and admiration for their captain as Chris prepared for the next game in his own unique ways. What was perceived one day as moody, selfish, and rude, became a source of respect. The behavior did not change — just the perception and understanding. These are twenty-year-old world-class athletes with an amazing amount of pressure to retain their World title and coached by some of the best technical advisors in the world. Yet they learned more from the tools of Colors about themselves, each other, and the values and strengths of their Green captain.

S.K.

(The names have been changed and the sport omitted. Yes, they did go on to repeat as World Champions.)

What You See Is Not What You Get

Talking with most Greens takes some special skills and a confident mind-set. Because of their neutral facial expressions, others may question if Greens are really listening. This is especially challenging for the people-first Blues and observant Oranges. Oranges are very visual and look for cues to determine the direction of conversations or presentations, and with Greens, there is very little to go on. Blues have an even harder time. Blues mirror emotions with their animated facial expressions. Talking with Greens can have Blues wondering whether they are talking too much (for most Greens they probably are), or whether the Green person is listening at all.

Yes, Greens are listening! In fact, they make some of the best listeners – as long as they believe there is value in the conversation, and it will be brief, be bright, and be gone. Greens absorb the information, evaluate every comment, and think through the implications. Their mental computer is on, and their notebook is open, and their pen is poised. They just don't value banter, preferring to sit and listen without interrupting.

Greens are not scary, mad, or cold, no matter their calm, cool demeanor and neutral expression. Their lack of a "friendly face" is almost always interpreted incorrectly. From Stephen Harper, Canadian Prime Minister who was continuously accused of having a "hidden agenda" by opposition parties, to Hillary Clinton's frequent descriptions as cold and uncaring, Greens are often wrongly assessed simply because of their lack of facial expression.

What people should know about me: Most people take my look as being mad. I'm not – it's just a look.

Profile on a dating website

Communicating with Greens is best done by focusing conversations on logic and facts. They prefer discussions that are well-articulated, concise, and to the point. Emotional conversations, excessive kidding around or redundant questions can quickly have Greens out of their comfort zone and tuned out.

Greens think of conversations and discussions almost like a tennis match. If the ball is in the other court, it's not their turn to talk. Then, as the ball is returned, there's a couple of seconds delay while they process the conversational volley and think ahead to what is really being asked. Finally they'll return the ball, responding with a few well-thought-out words. Greens respond to many questions with questions. This, together with their considerable vocabularies and wide-ranging interests, can be intimidating to others, often causing them to wish for the end of the game.

Respect is something to be earned from a Green, and it is never given away freely. They are not impressed by people-pleasers, or those who go along with something just for the sake of going along. They admire and value those who stand up for themselves and show the courage of their convictions. Confrontation is not really confrontation or conflict if someone brings the facts, knows their stuff, has done their homework, and can articulate their case. Any of those will get the attention and respect of Greens. And all the while, the Green person will be wondering what took them so long ...

Just Say No

Greens strive to make proper and correct decisions that are well thought out, accurate, and justifiable. When they are pressed for immediate answers, Greens will likely reply with a simple "No." What this no actually means is, "If you need an answer right now, without giving me the time to think about it, then the answer is no. (Now, go away.)"

Important questions with large implications require time to consider. Pushing Greens to come up with complex solutions off the top of their heads will not be successful. But, allowing Greens some built-in thinking time will result in well-informed decision-making. This approach also more frequently elicits a positive response, instead of the instinctive "no" to get the questioner off their case and out of their office.

This same mind-set applies during meetings, where Greens are irritated by decisions made without proper thought or adequate time to research options and alternatives. It is not about making a quick decision – it is about making the right decision. From staff meetings to planning their vacations, Greens need to have access to all the information well in advance, allowing them to be well-prepared, ask relevant questions, and contribute well-researched feedback and ideas in a meaningful way.

Greens are not people who shoot from the hip or talk without thinking: It just doesn't happen. Their thought process is logical, and once completed, you can be sure all opinions and options are solidly researched and defendable. At this point, their decision will stand until additional or better information is available, requiring them to revisit the issue.

Not to know is bad; not to wish to know is worse.

African Proverb

Pressure and Hype Equals Failure

Selling is not only about products or services. Each of us sells many times a day. We try to sell others on our point of view, on an idea, on our ideal vacation spot, or on the value of doing homework. In the world of sales, Greens do all of their research in advance. They would much rather be online than in line. When they do make a trip to the store it is only to obtain information they have not otherwise been able to get on the Internet. Greens then use the sales staff as their suppliers of missing information. It is not possible to sell something –anything – to a Green. To succeed with Green customers, as with a Green boss, a Green friend, or a Green co-worker, salespeople need to be credible and well-informed.

Many retailers have now identified Green shoppers, or rather, investigators. Green investigators focus on separating hype from reality. They avoid salespeople who have little credibility, and whose information is biased and inaccurate. Retail consulting firms have even given Greens a name, calling them *prosumers*. However, most retailers still have not learned how to deal with Greens, failing to understand that major purchases or critical decisions can well take a few months or more. Not to mention that Greens influence seven times as many people in their buying decisions as other Colors. But they are more than just research *shoppers*. Should they become seriously ill, Greens will diagnose themselves with the help of the Internet before walking into the doctor's office ... and will do so with their research on treatment options in hand.

The Drive for Perfection

Greens are on a lifelong journey to improve procedures and processes. They are well aware that perfection is a constantly moving target so it is not necessarily about reaching perfection, but about moving towards it. Greens are often a bit ahead of their time, and they see the world in very different ways, and they continually challenge others to keep growing, and to work towards how the world could be, rather than simply settling for what it is. They exert a powerful influence over others, and more often than not, they are the go-to people for problem solving and innovative solutions.

It can be frustrating for Greens when their suggestions are ignored, or their feedback does not result in change. Substandard results, the phrase "good enough" and obvious errors and flaws drive Greens nuts, and are a surefire way to get their backs up.

Anyone with Internet access is familiar with Wikipedia, the huge online, free encyclopedia with over twelve million entries. It was developed in 2001 by two friends as a site where everyone in the world could contribute articles, features and information in an open and unrestricted forum.

Larry Sanger was one of the original founders of Wikipedia. But after only two years, Sanger left the company when he started to question the accuracy and integrity of many entries and contributions. He walked away after disagreements with his partner as to whom should be allowed to contribute to the site, even before it became the giant it is today. It was never about money, fame or success for Sanger, but about credibility and doing it right.

In the words of Sanger himself, "Wikipedia began as a good-natured anarchy, a sort of Rousseauian state of digital nature. I always took Wikipedia's anarchy to be provisional and purely for purposes of determining what the best rules and the nature of its authority should be. What I, and other Wikipedians, failed to realize is that our initial anarchy would be taken by the next wave of contributors as the very essence of the project – how Wikipedia was 'meant' to be."

What did the Green Sanger do? He developed a better and more credible site and launched citizendium.org. This site has firm editorial rules and requires mandatory disclosure of the real names of its editors, whereas Wikipedia allows anyone with a user name to contribute untraceable content.

Paying It Forward

If you get sick, don't count on your Green friends to sit by your hospital bed for hours. It won't happen. But you can bet they will bring you some magazines, a new book, or a useful article from webmd.com. Why? Because you may as well use this time to read a good book, stimulate your mind, or learn something new.

Because of their own lifelong love of learning, Greens particularly appreciate the opportunity to teach and educate others – as long as they really want to learn. "You can't water a rock," a Green might say. A plant, on the other hand ...

Teaching others is the most tangible way Greens show the world that they care deeply. Unfortunately, their methods and style are often misunderstood, or may go unnoticed by other Colors. Greens seldom "dumb down" their teaching (that is how they see it), or simplify too many explanations:

> Before finishing her report, Gina e-mailed a friend for some graphics work. She also had a question about whether her friend thought the subtitle needed a comma. But for her Green friend, it wasn't just a question about one particular comma. It was an opportunity to teach Gina the comma's correct use:

> "A non-defining relative clause introduced by 'which' should be set off with a comma. Without it, it will be read as a defining clause (in which 'that' would be preferable as the relative pronoun). But I don't think this is what you want to imply here, my evidence being your choices to use the definite article and to capitalize the word ... in my opinion, the last bit has more of a problem than can be fixed by a comma, being what might be called a failed parallelism."

Green Discussions and Feedback

Greens believe the lifespan of small talk or idle chitchat should be less than a minute. But for anyone who values deep discussion, enjoys a good debate, or likes to be mentally challenged, Greens are always ready, willing, and more than able to participate. While their sharp minds and direct or blunt questions might seem intimidating, other Colors need to understand the Green approach as a compliment.

Greens only seriously pursue discussion or debate with someone for whom they have respect. After all, what's the point of a debate if the other person does not have anything valuable to contribute? Greens want to talk to people who have something to teach them – people who will challenge their mind.

It is important to remember that Green feedback is not criticism. When a Green person corrects someone, comments on, or points out errors, it is always from the mindset of wanting to provide better information. They are not looking for ways to shoot down ideas or to find fault. It is about caring enough to help others to learn, and to do better. To Greens, it is more important to be respected than liked, and more valuable to be knowledgeable than popular. Could Greens correct someone a little more gently, or less directly? Probably. But the approach should not negate the intent.

Greens will spend a lifetime impacting others. They can
certainly seem to be hard on people. Yet they are hard on
others exactly because they care, and want someone to be more,
to do better, to think more critically, and to always improve.

What You See and Hear From Greens

Greens are recognizable by their calm, cool, and collected demeanor, and their neutral expression. Other Colors may feel as though they are being evaluated by Greens, who can seem reserved and distant.

While clothing is just a necessity, and what to wear is not of great importance to Greens, the latest gadgets or computers are another matter. The Green workspace can be quite messy with their many projects and devices, not to mention their books, magazines, and manuals.

You'll hear a lot of "why?" and "how?" questions when you're listening to a Green. Pay attention! They don't like being asked to repeat themselves. They give logical, direct, and specific answers. Greens are people of few words, but their words are well-chosen, from a large vocabulary. Depending on the complexity of the issue, Greens may pause a few seconds to think before answering. The response may not be instant, but it will be accurate. Greens use humor and sarcasm and express themselves with "I think," and "I believe," instead of Blue "I feel" expressions.

Now I Understand...

Your need for Green time each day is not about me. It is not about being anti-social. It is time you reserve, and need, just for yourself.

Before I press you for an instant response, I should decide if I really need an answer now, or whether I value your well-thought-out responses.

You think things through properly and do nothing half-way. You look at the big picture and weigh all the options and possibilities. You take the time to see the whole puzzle while I may just be seeing a box of pieces.

With your easy-going nature, your feelings do run deeply. Just because they do not always come to the surface does not mean they are not real or do not exist.

I appreciate spending time with you, and it is not only about talking all the time. Sometimes the best communication with you is when you say nothing at all – just displaying your calm strength, logic, and demeanor.

Your Green face is not a way to measure your listening skills, or a scale to judge how much you care. Behind it is a great amount of caring and an ability to listen to me.

When you ask me a lot of questions, it is not a criticism of what I've said, but rather your never-ending desire to know more and more. It should not be a reason for me to become defensive, but an honor that you value learning something from me.

I am your boss or your friend. I am your partner, someone you work with or your relative ... and now I understand you a little better.

Common Green Strengths

Analytical and logical
Self-sufficient
Focusing
Problem solving
Independent and self-directed
Innovative
Asking great questions
Good teacher
Willing to tackle any problem
Holding high standards
Rational
Self-confident
Skeptical

Trustworthy
Happy to spend time alone
Future-oriented
Honest and direct
Visionaries
Inquisitive
Knowledgeable
Logical and factual
Even-tempered
Well-read
Direct
Witty
Taking nothing for granted

Common Green Stressors

Unfairness and injustice
Emotional outbursts
Incompetence
Insufficient information
Violation of personal space
Meetings with no point

Repetition and routine
Not knowing or understanding
Dishonesty in others
Irrational people
Quick decision-making
Rules that don't make sense

Deadlines
Forgetting something
Inconsistencies and redundancies
Interruptions
Illogic
No challenge or too much challenge
Doubt without justification
Not enough alone-time
People who don't value learning
Pushy salespeople
Having to rely on others
Spelling and grammatical errors

Chapter Six

Our Combinations of Colors

Life would be easier if all of us were just one personality type, giving us a simple, black-and-white view of the world. It would be easier, but it would also make our lives boring and one-dimensional.

Fortunately, nobody lives only in their primary Color. We are all, in different ways, at different times, and in different circumstances, made up of all of the four Colors. For many of us, for example, the way we need to act at work may be quite different from how we choose to act at home.

There is a time and a place for every action and for every Color – for all of us. We all know when it's time to have fun and play, and when it is critical to stop and think through an important decision. We all recognize there are occasions when it is crucial to be organized and at the same time would never hesitate to drop everything for a close friend needing help.

These are the values all four Colors share, but our strongest Color sets our priorities and shapes both how we see the world and how we would like it to work. The higher the score of your strongest Color, the more you will relate to the information in that Color chapter. Someone who has a close score between their first two Colors might pick and choose specific information from the two chapters.

No Color or combination of Colors is better than any other, but they are all certainly very different in the ways in which thoughts, behaviors, strengths, stresses, and values are manifested. What makes every person unique is our Color combination. Like a small jigsaw puzzle, we all have all four pieces, and for each of us, these puzzle pieces come in a unique combination of shapes and sizes which form our personality.

Our second Color plays a significant role in many of our behaviors, actions, values, and stresses. It is called our shadow Color – the part of our personality which lies in the shadow of the primary Color's motivators and strengths. This second Color exerts a strong influence.

A Blue second Color will remind us to be more patient and caring, and an Orange influence will let us know that it is OK to have fun and not take everything too seriously. A Green second Color provides a lifelong reminder to think things through and do it right the first time, while a Gold influence insists that we stay focused, structured, and on time.

Curt is a Blue/Gold Pastor. His first jobs after graduation were in the construction industry. The one thing that always horrified Curt was any project that did not have a complete set of blueprints. His high Gold and very low Orange did not want to just wing it, but needed clear and specific instructions. Long before he had ever heard of Colors, Curt always felt a drive to pursue a more people-oriented career. As a strong Christian, he soon realized his true calling was to be a Pastor.

The years at seminary were both richly rewarding and painfully difficult. His Blue intuition and faith instinctively knew that this was his true purpose in life. Likewise, his high Gold had made a plan and the thought of quitting before graduating was never an option. He had given his word and would see it through no matter what it took.

When Curt received his calling to a congregation, his primary job was leading the various youth groups and taking charge of the Sunday School. With his natural Gold planning and organizational skills, he was always prepared. From candy to activities, from stories to fun and games, the kids and their parents adored him. While Curt's Blue meant he loved working with people, the talents needed for dealing with high Orange kids were quite different to those required for working with adults. His strong core strengths of duty and serving conflicted with his desire to grow and to work in a less Orange area of the church.

Today Curt is Dean of Residence to over two hundred students at a very large Bible College. For Curt, it is a dream come true and a position which fully utilizes the gifts and strengths of his Blue/Gold.

Colors combine to help us make decisions, determine our actions and thoughts, and even set our priorities. The degree to which one or the other Color dominates, depends on the strength (score) of the shadow Color and the importance of the specific actions or decisions. A Gold/Green will often limit their research in order to get something finished and off their to-do list. The Green shadow Color would love to take the time to make the perfect decision, but the Gold drive for closure sets the time limit. For an Orange/Blue person, the Orange need for competition and victory is ever-present, but the Blue people-first influence will draw the line at bragging about the win. A Blue second Color will also resist team sports, where others could get hurt.

*Our primary and shadow Colors can either complement
each other or cause a clash between two different sets
of values. Whether consciously or not, these battles create
and shape us in many different ways.*

Our Different View of Others

We see situations, and even other people, in very different ways, depending on which Color we're "looking through." A simple staff meeting, for example, is not really simple, when for Golds, it's all about getting through the agenda in a disciplined manner and finishing on time, while Oranges are hoping to get out of there in less than 15 minutes. *PLEASE! Get to the point, make the decisions, and move on because we have real work to do.* Blues want to make sure that everyone gets a chance to feel included and heard, while Greens value some intelligent discussion, advance information, and the chance to think things through properly.

Even an everyday event, such as a traffic jam, can have our four Colors thinking in very different ways:

I was sitting in traffic, my 30 Gold score causing me to wait impatiently to get past an accident. At that point, my high Green score had me starting to wonder about the other drivers around me, and how their Colors determined how they reacted.

The Golds were likely in the lane furthest away from the wreck because you're supposed to move away from an accident, and they were in the lane they needed to be in, planning to make their exit a long way ahead. They were irritated that some people weren't moving to the open lane since there was a sign way ahead of the traffic warning everyone that there was an accident in the far left lane!

The Blues were probably in the next lane over so that they could help people move over away from the accident, but also in order to help people get on and off the exits. They were also in this lane so they would see the wreck to make sure no one was hurt or needed help. They had already dialed 911 and were waiting to press the "send" button in case help was needed. Perhaps the Greens were in the lane next to the accident in order to evaluate how many cars were in the wreck, how it happened and whose fault it was – all in an effort to at least learn something from this mess.

It's likely that the Orange drivers were in the accident lane until they just HAD to move over. Until then, it was the fastest moving lane. Of course, at the last minute they had to change lanes immediately and start inching forward without really waiting for someone to let them into the bumper to bumper traffic. Or perhaps they would be asked to stop and help direct traffic or something important?

It sure made waiting in traffic more fun. But I also had some questions: Would an Orange push into another lane because they were already late? Would they latch onto the next car's bumper to avoid letting anyone in since that would delay them an extra few seconds? Would Golds not let anyone in when they got close because they should have merged way back? Would a Blue be more likely to let you merge once you've made eye contact and (in a way) connected with them? Wouldn't this have been a great time to survey the Greens thinking through a more efficient way to handle this type of congestion? Or did many of them look around, wondering how stupid many other driver really were?

J.W.

Different is neither better or worse, nor right or wrong. For every instance that our Colors judge someone as being too... there are many others who think of us as just not being very... The tools of Colors allow us to look for the good in others and to appreciate their values and strengths. Without this understanding, our Colors will continually be labelled. To the world, there are always two opposing views of how we can see ourselves, and also the ways others might judge us:

Blues may see themselves as:	*Others may see Blues as:*
Affirming of others	Too nice/pushovers
Compassionate	Bleeding hearts
Creative	Not seeing the real world
Empathetic	Easily taken advantage of
Great communicators	Mushy
Idealistic	Naive
Liking to please	Not task oriented and easily side-tracked
A people person	Overly emotional
Romantic	Smothering
Social	Soft-hearted
Spiritual	Sugar-coating things
Trusting	Talking too much
Wanting harmony	Too trusting
Warm and caring	Unrealistic

Golds may see themselves as:

Abiding by policies
Always having a viewpoint
Business-minded
Reliable
Decisive
Efficient
Dependable
Goal-oriented
Great planners
Orderly and neat
Practical and stable
Providing security
Realistic
Steady and firm
Very organized

Others may see Golds as:

Single-minded
Bossy
Controlling
Uptight
Dull and boring
Dogmatic
Judgmental
Inflexible
Unimaginative
Opinionated
Predictable
Rigid
Stubborn
Stuck in the system

Oranges may see themselves as:

Even-tempered
Enjoying life
Flexible
Fun-loving
Great negotiators
Focused in the moment
Multi-taskers
Open to new ideas and suggestions
Practical
Problem-solvers
Resourceful
Spontaneous
Having a winning attitude

Others may see Oranges as:

Frequently late
Not serious
Rule-breakers
Scattered
Immoral
Flaky
Irresponsible
Manipulators
Problem creators
Not trustworthy
Unfeeling or uncaring
Unreliable
Renegades

Greens may see themselves as:	Others may see Greens as:
Able to reprimand	Aloof and cool
Always right	Arrogant
Calm under pressure	Cold
Creative	Controlled
Efficient	Uncaring
Exacting	Fault-finders
Firm-minded	Hatchet people
Logical decision-makers	Heartless
Rational	Intellectual snobs
Seeking justice	Lacking mercy
Superior intellectually	Loners
Thorough thinkers	Ruthless
Objective	Unfeeling
Unique and original	Unrealistic

Everyday we judge other people and form opinions about them based on our own criteria and values and how we see them through the filters of our Colors. But if we believe that people come into our lives for a reason, we are ahead of the game already, and open to appreciating other Colors' strengths and contributions. Is someone cold and aloof, or are we prepared to view valuable Greens in much more positive ways?

Meeting an Orange person, someone full of energy and talking very quickly, what tends to be our first thought? What about the people at work, focused intensely on their current project? Do we think of them as uncaring and task-oriented? Or are we prepared to see them as focused, responsible, and invaluable? Do we perceive our Blue friends as always having the time for others and genuinely caring? Or in the office, is our initial reaction that there is too much talk and not enough work? Beauty is always in the eye of the beholder.

Facebook question: OK, tell me: How do you get ready for a trip? Do you have a long to-pack list, and pull the suitcases out two days before, or what?

List starts a month in advance and re-written at least a few times. Packing starts three weeks before the trip. Anything less and I'd be in a sheer panic!

C.C.W. – Gold/Blue

What's a list? And do you really expect me to find it when I need it? I seem to have rule-following issues, never mind list things…

P.J.G. – Orange/Green

My husband is a Green. Long lists of things "we may need" like batteries, torches, matches, etc. Not that we go anywhere that we would need them! Plenty of "over thinking" it to my Orange mind!

L.N. – Orange/Blue

I have a long to-pack list and pack days before we leave. My hospital bag (when I was pregnant) was packed months in advance!

N.B.G. – Gold/Blue

I have a long mental to-pack list … but pull my suitcase out 30 minutes before I leave.

SELR – Green/Orange

I pack passport, tickets, and clothes a week before so I don't wear them again. Night before, I unpack everything because I've forgotten what I packed. Then I re-pack. List? No point. I'd forget where I put it.

S.M.H – Blue/Orange

We are going on holidays in four months. I've started my list a week ago, the same time we booked the trip!

K.P. – Gold/Blue

Start way ahead but then it's 50-50 whether I can find the right box it's in. Sometimes I have to go on a hunt. I do get the suitcase out the day before while I'm realizing I have laundry to do, and hope I don't have to pack wet clothes.

B.H.Y. – Orange/Green

I make a list a few days out and make it for the whole family and always add to it. I seem to have trigger items on it that trigger off a whole raft of specific items, like following the branches of a mind map. I even pack for my husband, the right way. But he unpacks and re-packs at which point I have to walk away …

S.P. – Green/Orange

I love having a packing list. I also have items like extra toiletries that I've bought to leave packed and at the ready for packing! I do all the packing for the four of us, so lists are a must. Because, if I forget anything, I'd hear about it. And that is definitely not good for my Blue feelings.

T.H.Mc. – Blue/Gold

You mean to tell me you'd know, or remember, you're going somewhere two days before you leave?

M.W. – Orange/Blue

List? If my mental list counts, then yes. Pack two days before? Never. But I've done the mental planning the week before as to what I'm wearing …

J.J.D. – Green/Gold

*Love writing a list, but then lose it…but it doesn't bother me
… it's part of the excitement.*

R.H. – Blue/Orange

*I'm leaving for Orlando in three weeks. The suitcase is in the
bedroom and ready. The written list is on the computer, which
includes things like oil change for the car, stop the mail, turn
off air or heat, etc. Laundry is this week, for things that will be
ironed and set aside for packing. Dining room table will soon
accumulate puzzles and games to take along.*

T.K. – Green/Gold

Our Shared Strengths and Values

We are all made up of a unique combination of Colors, but the Colors
themselves do share some common ground. Learning about those
shared traits and feelings is much more valuable than focusing on
our differences. With an open heart and mind, it's easy to find ways
in which we are more alike than different.

Blue and Orange

These are two people-first Colors who draw their energy from
others and believe that paperwork will never be as important as their
team, their friends, their co-workers, or their clients. Drop a Blue or
an Orange in a new city, and by the next day they will have made
some new friends. Oranges can talk to anyone about anything, at a
party or a networking event, while Blues prefer one-on-one
conversations where they can really get to know someone.

As natural optimists, both automatically look for the positive in
things. They are both very generous, and they're great motivators
who avoid negative people and situations whenever possible. They

prefer to tackle things hands-on, rather than just talking about them. Both Colors are also talented negotiators, albeit in different ways. Oranges succeed in life through their drive to win and by thinking on their feet, while Blues use their intuition and their special talent to build meaningful relationships.

Blues and Oranges use humor to keep things positive. They're creative, and both believe strongly in dreaming the impossible dream. They value recognition, and shine brighter when they receive genuine, positive feedback for their unique talents and contributions. For Oranges, tangible rewards work best, while their Blue friends prefer heartfelt words of affirmation and praise.

Gold and Green

If something needs to be done, it's going to be done right if Golds and Greens are involved. These two Colors are process-oriented and value logical and efficient ways of doing things. (If others have a better idea, they will need to be able to prove that it's better.) Both naturally think ahead, planning for any potential challenges, pitfalls, missing details, or problems. If anything does go wrong, they can be quite unforgiving. They are hardest on themselves.

Because Golds and Greens believe that their actions and achievements speak to their credibility, any job they take on will almost certainly be done correctly. Both Colors focus intensely on the task at hand and prefer to work in a quiet area without interruptions. Golds want to get the job done so they can legitimately cross it off their to-do list, while Greens need to do it perfectly the first time before they can comfortably move on to something else.

Both Golds and Greens value their privacy and prefer others to get to the point, since neither have much time for small talk. They are task-oriented, both in overall outlook and behavior, and they often have the tendency to put the job to be done ahead of the people involved.

It is not possible to tell from their expressions what is really going on with them. Golds and Greens are often accused of not "looking" happy: Greens tend to be calm and cool, while Golds generally have a concerned or focused demeanor.

Green and Orange

On the surface it might not seem that most Orange extroverts and Green introverts could possibly have much in common. Yet both are very independent and strong-minded. Neither have a problem challenging authority – they don't want to be told what to do or how to do it. These Colors share an "I can do it" attitude and tremendous amount of self-confidence.

Neither Greens nor Oranges beat around the bush. They speak their minds in pretty direct ways, without a lot of tolerance for small talk. They don't mean to hurt feelings, and they don't understand that they often do. Oranges will admit they frequently speak before thinking, while Greens have trouble seeing how someone can be "hurt" by facts and honest feedback. (It's not logical!)

Problem solving is a sport for both of these Colors, who enjoy competition and new challenges. They're happy to compete with anyone, anytime. Oranges see competition as a way to stay motivated – to keep things interesting and exciting. Greens aren't interested in basking in the limelight, as many Oranges are. For them it's all about the mental stimulation and knowing they can do it. Their true preference is to compete with themselves or with systems of some kind.

Oranges and Greens love setting – and reaching! – new goals, and they avoid mundane and repetitive tasks whenever possible. Both need space to perform and are eager to seek new ways and methods of doing things: Oranges motivated by the desire to avoid boredom and routine, and Greens by the drive to improve and to utilize their ingenuity. Oranges find shortcuts while Greens map out a more efficient route.

Gold and Blue

Golds and Blues share a common need: to help others. They make up the vast majority of volunteers, and are generous with their time and money, working tirelessly for charities and worthy causes. Helping their fellow man and lending a hand gives them a strong sense of belonging and feeling valued, while raising their self-esteem. These motivations, to help others and to treat others as they wish to be treated, make Golds and Blues terrific team players. They instinctively act for the greater good. They are very protective of their friends and families and share a strong sense of loyalty.

Golds and Blues both have a hard time saying no to anyone, yet both also find it very difficult to ask for help themselves. That somehow seems selfish, and they do not want to impose.

For both, conflict of any kind is to be avoided at all costs. They are rule followers who very much value fitting in above making waves or standing out. They are receptive though, to expressions of appreciation. As very modest Colors, neither wants others to make a big deal over them, but they don't want to be forgotten, either. Expressions of thanks and gratitude will be remembered and cherished.

Green and Blue

While Greens embrace logic and Blues live in their hearts, these two seemingly dissimilar Colors do share some strong bonds, one of the major ones being their great creativity. For Greens, this creativity is most often manifest in their talent for improving systems and procedures, while Blues express themselves in a wide range of artistic areas.

There is a beautiful movie called *Pay It Forward* which illustrates the powerful ways in which Blues may make a difference in the lives of others. Greens have that same need to help, but they do so in different ways, most particularly through sharing their love of learning with others. To Greens, the best way to show someone you care and want to help is to teach them something. Both Greens and Blues wish to leave their mark on the world by having a positive impact on the lives of others.

Both value a focus on the big picture. They readily see all sides of an issue – Greens with their lateral thinking skills, and Blues as consummate and empathetic mediators.

A continuous challenge for these two Colors is to look forward. Whether the tendency is to constantly rethink and reevaluate past decisions, or to relive lingering hurt feelings, Blues and Greens need to be mindful that they can not change the past. This issue is compounded for anyone with Blue and Green as their highest Color combination.

Gold and Orange

Golds and Oranges would always rather act instead of talk. They can be impatient, wanting to just get on with it: "Tell me what to do and let me do it." Both live in the moment and prefer to focus on the job at hand without wasting time and energy on long range ideas and visions, but they also both work well in teams. Golds contribute by helping others out of a sense of duty and need to get the job done, while Oranges make things happen with their people-oriented nature, their enthusiasm, and their flexibility. Now if others could just share their drive …

On the surface it might seem that these two Colors would have very different definitions of friendship. Oranges have lots of friends and even more acquaintances, while Golds tend to have just two or three lifelong friends. But for Oranges, who seem to know everyone, there are few people who truly know *them* in a meaningful way. Golds appear to be very private people – and they are – but the same is true for Oranges.

Both Golds and Oranges value being in charge and in control: Oranges because of their strong, center-of-attention personalities and Golds because of their iron-clad definitions of what is right and wrong. Both measure their successes in large part through money, even though they totally disagree on what to do with it after they have earned it.

The Journey for Balance

The power which comes from understanding the tools and insights of Colors is personal and varied. Perhaps it comes from putting words and definitions to things we always knew, but never had the words to express or describe. The most important thing though, is to have an open heart and mind and to always look for the value and the good in others, choosing to see other Colors as a gift and a blessing.

All of us naturally see the world through the eyes of our Colors. For the majority of people, living life in balance requires patience, practice, and a willingness to look at things a little differently. It comes from a desire to do more of what works, and less of what doesn't, in our lives. To:

- Understand our strengths and know which of them we tend to take to extremes, where they have the potential to be a problem instead of a blessing.

- Always remember the unique values and joys within other Colors. Take the time to communicate and appreciate these other Colors on their terms and in ways they value and understand.

- Be mindful that most people do not share our personality type, and at times, their words, actions, and behaviors are not as ours would be. We need to be conscious of our judgments and reactions at such times.

We cannot control or change others, their actions or reactions. We can, however, teach them about Colors, and the preferences and challenges inherent within each Color. Nobody chooses to annoy us on purpose. When we all understand each other a little bit better, our Color conflicts will be greatly minimized, and our relationships will improve.

Could you, or are you willing to, stretch yourself today? Can you do something today which is a little out of your Color's comfort zone? The challenge is to do one thing a little differently. Something small enough that you actually do it, but large enough that you will notice the change.

Nothing that you learn about Colors will, or should, change you. Each of us is unique and special, and a first-rate version of who we are. We should never attempt to become a second-rate version of someone else. But there is a time and a place for everything and for every Color's strengths. Living a life in balance means embarking on a journey of growth and self-improvement.

Your Blue consistently shows in your caring for and reaching out to others. You involve everyone around you and give from the heart — to your friends, to your family, and to others. Your kindness and communication skills touch everyone you come in contact with. Your genuine warmth, empathy, and teamwork skills are contagious and positively impact those around you. You make lasting friendships and are always ready, willing, and able to make time for others.

Your Gold stands out in your loyalty, dependability, and special talent in taking on tasks and seeing them through to completion. Your strong sense of right and wrong and your strong work ethic means you meet deadlines and work well without supervision, both on your own and as a team player. People can always count on you to help wherever and whenever you're needed.

Your Orange is evident in your energy level, and the positive outlook that others admire. You have a contagious sense of humor and through your practicality and high energy level, you show others that anything is possible. Your ability to multi-task without feeling stressed and your flexibility are valued and envied by those who see you in action. You are never afraid to roll up your sleeves and get involved.

Your Green pursues challenges and solutions, constantly seeking improvements while keeping your eye on the big picture and broader vision. Your range of knowledge goes far beyond your job, and it is well-known and respected. You continue to learn and to grow, always seeking opportunities to share your knowledge, ideas and suggestions with others.

To summarize:

> Embrace yourself as you are ...
> Just for today —
> make your Gold lists shorter,
> nurture your Blue relationships,
> value and grow your Green knowledge,
> and treasure your Orange freedom.

Sure, we have lots in common — like that we're both impatient.
I want to get it done and off my list and you want
to get it done because you're bored.

I know you're concerned and nervous, but when I said we should
talk, I just meant about my dreams and feelings and stuff.

Chapter Seven

Relationships: Love is Colorblind

I'll go and get it.
I'll come along.
What if I just want to go by myself?
Sorry, you gave that up when we got married, dear.

Opposites attract. More than half of all couples are in a relationship with a partner of a totally different Color. Consciously or unconsciously, we are often drawn to someone who has the skills and strengths we lack. We are attracted to those whose personality traits complement ours, creating a strong bond: *We can do anything if we just do it together.*

A loving and healthy relationship is like a little piece of heaven right here on earth. Yet healthy relationships do not happen by accident. They require commitment, effective communication and hard work – the many tools and building blocks two people must use to grow together as a couple. While Colors is not a dating how-to, it can be another of those tools, helping to create a deeper understanding of our partner's strengths, stressors, and values. What we see of our potential partners through our Colors knowledge really will be what we get.

But what do we want from our relationships? Which traits do we most admire in our partners, and which actions, behaviors or inactions create stress? Knowing is always better than hoping. Our partners are not going to "come around," change their Colors, or somehow transform themselves into different people – people more like us.

Could that wish to "change" our partner be a contributory factor to the increasing divorce rate? Is there some time in the first, or fifth, or tenth year of marriage when one partner starts to spend most of their relationship energy on "helping" their partner become more like themselves? When all we can think about is "fixing" our partner's behaviors, it's a dangerous and slippery slope.

For second marriages, the divorce rate is even higher. So the second time around, we make worse relationship decisions? Yes, opposites attract, but more often than not, we do not have a true understanding of what that means – and we need to.

Whom does each Color tend to marry? While the chart below is not definitive, the survey results are from sufficiently large numbers of seminar attendees and have significant validity.

Partner's Primary Color

Primary Color	Green	Gold	Orange	Blue
Gold	22%	27%	24%	27%
Orange	43%	12%	24%	21%
Blue	24%	30%	14%	32%
Green	29%	27%	38%	6%

Who do we date or marry? Challenges can arise in any
relationship, regardless of our partner's Colors. Will we
remember the beautiful traits that first attracted us? Will we
still value them years from now? Is love colorblind?

Honest, open, and effective communication is, and always will be, one of the most important building blocks in a successful relationship. Spending quality time together and honest communication are the most frequently cited attributes of healthy relationships.

If communication is one of the key factors for growth, it can also be a prime area of conflict. "I communicate really well, it's just that my partner doesn't." How often do we want to be right, instead of happy? Or choose to speak only in the language of our own Colors, instead of communicating in ways our partner actually values and understands? Can doing the same thing over and over ever produce a different result?

Many times, seemingly simple conversations with our different-Color partner quickly escalate. It may not seem like a big deal at the time, but hurt feelings linger, and the battle lines are drawn. Oranges may raise their voices in frustration or make fun of something or someone. For them, it's meaningless and is quickly forgotten. Their Gold or Green partner however, may take that criticism as a personal attack.

Blues, the vast majority of whom are women, may feel frustrated, unheard, or unloved when their husbands – primarily Greens and Golds – don't understand what they really want or mean. These Gold and Green men are comfortable fixing and solving – hearing and understanding can be a challenge. Bridging the gap between, "If you loved me you would know," and, "What exactly do you want me to do?" takes true insight and commitment.

As the above relationship combinations show, love truly is Colorblind. While that seems like great news, the skyrocketing divorce rate makes it clear that we need instead to see and acknowledge the real Colors of our partners.

Do You Have the Time?

Each and every day we take the time to get ourselves ready in the morning. We take the time to shower, get dressed to look good, and take care of ourselves. Every day we make the time for work, to go out with our friends, and to watch our favorite television shows.

We choose to make the time to learn a new sport or hobby. We take two, three, or four years to earn our degree. We invest years at work to earn a promotion, almost two decades to raise our kids, and even longer to save for our retirement.

But somehow we often take our relationships for granted and expect them to grow stronger without effort. Invest the time – use the tools of Colors – and spend the same amount of energy on your relationship as you do in other areas of your life. It is worth it, your partner is worth it, and it will be one of the best investments you make.

The Rainbow of Relationship Combinations

What is the best combination of Colors to have in a relationship? The answer is simple: exactly the unique combination each couple has. Every relationship combination includes a long list of gifts and strengths along with its challenges. That being said, an understanding of Colors will contribute in a multitude of ways to any couple's becoming a loving and unstoppable team. All that is needed is an open heart, an open mind, and the willingness to learn and grow together.

When two people enter into a relationship, they are combining two distinct personalities. Some merge easily, while others require more flexibility, but every combination benefits greatly from looking at the world through the eyes of each other's Colors. Focusing less on changing, and more on creating an understanding between spouses, is a powerful tool, and the foundation for building an enduring, healthy relationship.

Blue and Gold: Doing it right or feeling good about it?

Blue and Gold are an extremely common couple combination. This pairing can be a beautiful balance between getting the job done and caring about others. Remember, these two Colors make up the largest groups of volunteers. They both believe strongly in giving back, by sharing their time, their talents, and their money.

This couple places a priority on family and friends. Golds may have a small group of three or four lifelong friends, while their Blue partners may have many more, but they both share a huge sense of loyalty towards them. More reserved Golds are often amazed at, and admire, how easily their partners can make so many genuine friends so quickly.

The Blue gift for giving, caring, and sharing unconditionally is something their Gold partner also admires. Golds appreciate that their Blues love them for who they are, not for what they do and whether or not they meet their own self-imposed high expectations or lofty standards. Blues will soften the Gold drive to work harder and to do more. They know that happiness is a journey, not a Gold destination.

At first this may be a challenge for Golds to accept since, in their view, hard work and a completed to-do list equals success, and success equals happiness. They worry a lot and are constantly working to make sure that everything gets done, that they are saving enough, that things are planned, that they are a good enough parent. It might be great to hear their Blue partner say not to worry, or that it's no big deal, but Golds will need to hear it often before they really hear it. Even love is something some Golds feel needs to be earned, while to every Blue, love is unconditional, regardless of accomplishments, failures or setbacks.

How powerful for Golds, to know that their Blue partners will always put people and feelings first, even at the expense of their own needs and feelings. It is give-and-take: This is where Golds can be a great help to their Blues by setting boundaries, saying no, and making sure their Blue partners take care of themselves first.

Setting boundaries, or just being direct and to-the-point, is easy for Golds. They have no trouble saying, "Tomorrow we need to ..." It is much harder for Blues and their "We should maybe ..." Golds are action-oriented. A "we should" will have Golds out of their seat and starting to move. An understanding of each other's communication methods highlights the value of compromise. There is room between direct and oblique. Until it is reached though, Blues will sometimes get frustrated, feeling as if they're never heard nor understood.

The Blue partner is more of a big-picture dreamer and much more creative. The Blue-Gold relationship will grow in measurable ways when Golds use their practical skills and process-oriented views to foster and support their partner's big dreams, however unrealistic those dreams may seem to them. In return, Blues will offer a people-first view and some creative options to the Gold black-or-white mindset and decision-making style.

Green and Blue: Think it through or feel it?

When Green and Blue are together, living by the heart and living through logic co-exist. While Green and Blue both value the stability of their committed relationship, their specific traits and values shine through. The Blue partner is the caregiver as well as the caretaker and heart of the relationship. He or she will remember birthdays, anniversaries and social occasions. The Blue partner will also build a very close relationship with his or her in-laws, who may be unaccustomed to such close and personal attention from their Green son or daughter.

Blues will most likely take on the majority of the housework, shopping, and other chores that help make a house feel more like a home. Many of these are things Greens enjoy having done for them, even though at times they may not understand their importance. Blues take many things off their Green partner's plate – things important to a healthy relationship. Without their Blue partners, Greens often give little thought to regular meals, buying new clothes, or keeping up with the housework.

Blues allow their Green partners to remain focused on the bigger issues and not have to deal with the daily needs and tasks they perceive to be tedious and mundane. When it comes to things like hosting dinner parties or spending time with friends and family, it will be the Blues who make things happen.

A Green's need for some alone-time every day is sometimes difficult for Blues to understand. (It may take a while for the Blue partner to stop feeling as though they have done something wrong.) But Blues are very proud of the intelligence and calm demeanor of their partners. Their Green is truly someone they can lean on, someone who will help to set the boundaries. Their partners can also be helpful in finding simple and logical solutions, and can shrink blown-out-of-proportion problems back down to size.

Greens are people of few words who prefer to deal with logic and facts. Do not expect them to speak freely – from their hearts – without filtering and considering their words first. That is the Blue way. Greens will always speak factually and logically, which may result in hurt feelings. Yet these comments are made because Greens love their Blue partners, because they want them to do better, think better, and have better information; they are never intended to be hurtful. Greens do love to learn though, and their relationships will grow stronger if they study and begin to use some of the softer Blue communication tools.

Greens love to study people. They are pattern-seekers who often understand their Blue partners better than their partners seem to know themselves. But until they understand – and perhaps even modify their own behavior – they will continue to puzzle over how quickly feelings can get hurt, why simple things are taken to heart, and why going along just to get along can be such a priority to a Blue.

Finally, as important as an hour of alone-time is for Greens, four hugs a day are even more critical for Blues. Physical touch, cuddling on the sofa, holding hands and hugs are not optional: They are as critical as air is to breathing. Blues will sometimes nag to get a Green to understand their need for affection, but at that point they sometimes also refuse the physical closeness. It may not seem logical, but Blues need their Green partners to want to want it, not to do so out of a sense of obligation. When affection is an integral part of their daily life, Blues will feel loved beyond anything logic can express.

Orange and Gold: Should we wing it or make a plan?

Opposites attract, and this couple is proof! They are a powerful combination: a flexible, eternally optimistic Orange multi-tasker, together with a serious Gold who will take care of the planning and structure. Oranges contribute their ideas and creativity, along with their positive energy and networking skills. Their Gold partners are happy out of the limelight, behind the scenes, taking care of the details.

With so much going on, Oranges are very grateful for their Golds. Someone needs to do that stuff – and it better not be them. So as long as paperwork and structure are not required from them, as long as nothing takes away from their need for freedom or imposes a lot of "have to" rules, Oranges will gladly let their Gold partners handle the details.

Golds value their Orange partners' hands-on skills, flexibility, and ability to work well under stress. They marvel at Oranges' *No Fear* and *Just Do It* attitudes, consistently positive outlook, and inability to take no for an answer. Golds watch Oranges try almost anything, often without a firm plan, and are often left shaking their heads in amazement. It can actually be a little embarrassing for Golds, but they are so proud of their Orange partners' talents.

As we all know, there is a time and a place for everything, but in the Gold-Orange partnership, issues of flexibility versus planning can often arise. Golds may have their whole Saturday mapped out, but if something better comes along, will they be willing to stay flexible and change plans? After dinner, when Oranges are restless and need to *do something right now*, can they give Golds thirty minutes to load the dishwasher, clean up the kitchen, and complete their to-do list? And can Golds remember to make it clear that their partner is more important than doing the dishes *right now*?

When there is compromise between living for the moment and planning every minute, the relationship will flourish and grow. Some vacation planning, for example, is necessary and valuable. But any Orange will have more fun getting there, getting lost, and exploring places than following a fixed agenda. What a joy it is to learn together that not worrying and being happy is fun, just as staying on track and having a plan before jumping in can sometimes help avoid headaches and costly mistakes. Many times, one person will see opportunities, while the other sees the pitfalls. When both can explain and share their points of view, they become a much stronger team.

The Gold-Orange couple enjoys making money. Where they differ is in deciding whether this money should be saved and invested or spent on material things. It is through trial and error (and definitely an argument or two) that they will find a workable compromise, somewhere between the Orange impulse-shopping style of *see it – want it – buy it*, and the Gold need to find a good deal, comparison shop, and put away savings for that guaranteed-to-come rainy day. Golds are quite conservative with money, while Oranges believe there will always be more where that came from.

Green and Orange: Just do it or think about it?

Both Greens and Oranges are very independent, but in very different ways – something they discovered about each other on their first date. Greens never want to be told what to think, and Oranges have no patience for anyone who tries to tell them what to do.

For Greens, Oranges are a kind of mystery to be studied and solved. Their partners are the outgoing, active, and impulsive ones in the relationship. They network with anyone and everyone, and thrive on a life rich in social interactions. Greens are constantly amazed. In the Green world, parties would be best few and far between, and speaking without thinking does not happen. And outgoing? Not so much. Their differences are clear: At a party, Oranges are looking to meet a dozen different people whom they can enlist for a fundraiser or who might become future clients, while their Green partners have wandered off in search of someone who can discuss the validity of Neuro-linguistic programming.

Oranges quickly realize that large parts of their social life may happen without their spouse, who prefers to stay home with a good book or a new computer application. For Greens, alone time is a treat, while for Oranges, it's more like a punishment. The push to *go do something* usually starts with the Orange partner, although what they actually *go do* includes things of interest to their Green partner too.

Oranges may often speak first and think later. They shoot from the hip and develop ideas while talking them through. When these creative and off-the-cuff ideas are filtered through the mind of their Green partner though, they may be amended, fixed, fleshed-out, and perfected. What a perfect combination: creative ideas and intellectual analysis.

When they work together it's wonderful, but Oranges sometimes need to remember that their partners are not killing their ideas or vision. When Greens correct spelling, grammar, or ideas, it is not about criticism or control; it is about love. Greens want their partners to have better information, to sound more credible, and to make better decisions.

Making better decisions extends to what to wear and how to shop as well. Oranges tend to love the latest, coolest fashions, while Greens place little value on something which to them seems trivial. They can't see spending time thinking about what to wear – just put something on! But if they're thinking about buying a new car or laptop, well that is worth spending time on. Not the 15-minute in-and-out Orange shopping trip, but research and reading before even heading to the store. Compromise is key, but it's more likely that a Green will be able to speed up than it is that an Orange will be able to slow down.

Gold and Green: Take it off the list or make it perfect?

This couple is task-oriented, responding to issues with concrete actions and quality work, leading to tangible results and a great sense of accomplishment. People and their feelings may take a back seat to getting the job done, and done right.

Golds benefit greatly from their Green partner's love of learning and ability to find more efficient solutions and see more than one possibility. They share the typical Green calm demeanor when they're able to stop stressing over small issues and focus on the big picture rather than just to their to-do lists.

In return, Golds help to keep their Green partners grounded by viewing life in realistic terms and coming up with practical solutions. Without their support, Greens could be "thinking things through" indefinitely. When Golds force a resolution, Greens can be more relaxed – even passive – in the relationship, letting Golds be the on-the-go partner with definite ideas of what needs to be done and when.

But should "what needs to be done" be done now, or done perfectly? Whether it is a home renovation project or a financial overhaul, this question may be problematic. To Golds, once something has been decided and is on their to-do list, it needs to be finished – now! The primary motivation is to get the job done. This is not a Green goal. Tinkering, experimenting, taking time to research options, and getting feedback at the home improvement store, can make any project fun and rewarding. It can also ensure that it is done right, even if it takes longer than anticipated.

It is for this reason that the Gold partners will likely be the ones who take care of the practical, daily tasks, such as shopping, cleaning, and cooking. Thanks to Golds, parties and family celebrations are planned well in advance, with no details left to chance. Gifts are bought, wrapped, and sent on time – every time. Greens know all these things should be important, but they are seldom a priority. Thank goodness for their Gold partners!

While Golds define organization as neat piles and labeled boxes, Greens believe strongly in mental organization. So it helps when Greens have their own space somewhere in the house. The expression "everything in its place" is not one Greens embrace, and this can drive their Gold partners nuts. Greens also need a place to spend their alone time, get on the computer, read, or just relax. Alone time is an absolute must, so Golds must be careful not to act as though this Green time is something to be earned after their real to-do list is finished.

Orange and Blue: Get over it or let the feelings linger?

These two people-first Colors care deeply about their relationships. Blues' self-esteem is tied to their emotions, their feelings of intimacy and affection, and the meaningful relationships they share. They always make time for others. Their Orange partners have a large circle of friends, never getting too bogged down in the emotions of the relationships.

Blues are frequently drawn to the Orange sense of humor and their ability to quickly and painlessly leave the past in the past, but at times this may cause conflict, when Blues feel their Orange partners do not take their feelings seriously enough, or understand their need to relive events, conversations, or hurt feelings. It's true: Oranges do not always understand why Blues cannot just get over it and get on with life. Life is too short! Blues can sometimes misinterpret this as uncaring.

Oranges want to be taken at face value, and they treat others the same way. They seldom linger over hidden meanings or listen for what is not being said. If they do not understand something, or want to know more, they will ask a direct question. This can make their Blue partners cringe, even though they might admire the ability to cut to the chase and get to the point. It's something that's hard for Blues to do, and sometimes it's may be perceived as rude. Blues analyze conversations, searching for deeper meanings or the real feelings behind the words. But they often do appreciate that the Oranges' directness leaves much less room for misunderstandings. The great benefit is that Blues can learn to become more direct while helping their Orange partners become more aware of feelings and emotions. Blues can act as Oranges' early-warning system, alerting them when feelings are hurt or when patience and sensitivity is needed.

In an Orange-Blue relationship, Blues have someone who can set boundaries for them and say "no" where they just can't. Blue intuition lets them know that their partners love them and care for them deeply, even if they have a really hard time talking things through without getting sidetracked, cracking a joke, or bottom-lining the conversation.

The challenge for Blues is to not make their Orange partners feel trapped or confined. When Oranges experience this boxed-in feeling, it is possible that they will want to leave the relationship entirely.

Blues look for quality time with their Orange partners, cuddling on the sofa or holding hands. Since these require Oranges to stop multi-tasking, Blues need to create opportunities for these times in healthy, win-win ways. If Blues appear needy or clingy, Oranges may start tuning them out in and distancing themselves on purpose in order to protect their need for freedom. When their partners feeling are then hurt, it only compounds matters. Blues have deep-seated feelings and emotions; they look for the good in everyone and will continually forgive. But they will not easily forget, and having their feelings hurt too often may result in their building up walls in order to protect themselves.

Both Orange and Blue likely have people-first jobs and can become hugely successful using their natural, relationship-building skills. Since neither enjoys the mundane in life, things are a lot easier at home when this couple is able to hire someone else to do their housework, their taxes, and their investment management. Someone has to – it just should not be either of these two Colors, unless their second color is a strong Gold.

Gold and Gold: *Taking care of business*

This relationship likely started as a friendship, and this Gold-Gold couple probably dated for a long time before making a commitment. Neither partner would likely jump into a relationship without an extended test-drive, without getting to know one another really well, often over a number of years. Once in a relationship, this is definitely the get-it-done team. Together these two will accomplish anything they set their minds to, with focus and an unwavering determination. Both are primarily task-oriented and prefer to plan, execute, and move on. There is not any additional discussion or wasted time when they are on task and on the job.

The Gold-Gold partnership finds comfort and security in the tried and true, established routines of their lives. It may not seem like fun to others, but for these two it is. Once all the work is done – a neat and organized home, the yard work finished, the bills paid – then it's time to relax, have fun, and enjoy themselves.

Both partners have strong leadership skills and prefer to be the decision-makers in the relationship. Neither likes to be told what to do or to be presented with a ready-made decision. Their disagreements are not so much about what needs to get done, but more about how to do it and the order in which it should be accomplished. Most of the time, Gold couples prefer a clear and specific division of duties, particularly around the house, which helps prevent these disagreements. Of course they will help each other, but at the end of the day, someone does need to be accountable, responsible, and in charge.

Learning to share duties and responsibilities, and to be open to the wishes of their partners, are valuable lessons this Gold team must learn. One partner may sometimes exhibit a few traits which seem to go against the Gold nature. They may be defaulting to their second

Color as another way to feel in control. This can range from being late, to not finishing tasks or projects.

It is likely that both partners are involved with a service club, their church, a community group, or charity. Golds make up the largest group of volunteers and feel an obligation to give back to society. That obligation, together with a strong sense of duty and responsibility, may be the reason they first volunteered, but when Golds contribute their time and talents they are also rewarded with a sense of purpose and belonging.

Golds are very good with money and savings. They share conservative and traditional values and feel safe and loved knowing that they can trust each other unconditionally. They are always true to their word and honor their promises. Golds strongly believe in traditions and the institution of marriage – for better or worse, and definitely until death do us part – no matter what.

Orange and Orange: The power couple makes it happen

Action-packed and adventure-filled are words most often used to describe this power couple's relationship. Unlike their Gold friends' lengthy dating history, these two most likely sped through the process – a lot. Their ability to make quick decisions certainly came into play. It's the Orange energy, networking skills, and need to always be on the go – times two! Others will be hard-pressed to keep up with them.

Both partners are game to try almost anything and everything, living life by their own rules. Within every relationship, our second Color matters a lot, and that is especially true in this Orange-Orange partnership. An Orange/Gold partner will want to play, but will also be in charge of making up the rules. A Blue second Color will be more sensitive to hurt feelings and act cautiously instead of speaking first and then dealing with the fallout later. And an Orange/Green partner will quickly switch from making impulse decisions to striving for perfectionism, needing to have a certain amount of alone-time and becoming more self-critical.

Oranges believe competition is healthy, and that it leads to success. In their Orange-Orange partnership, they've someone close by to put up a good fight and motivate them. Almost everything, from sports to conversations to housework, can become a contest. Together, they feed off each other's competitive drive and winning attitude. "What can go wrong?" "We can do anything!"

With the strong Orange desire for freedom, at least one partner will likely be self-employed, or have some type of sales or commission-based career. Both will use their networking skills and vast circle of friends to become successful. Oranges know how to spend, so this success will necessarily be financial as well. This team is all about working hard and playing hard, enjoying the freedom that financial success brings to come and go as they please. They are very generous, but money comes and goes quickly, spent on toys, cars, clothes, and eating out.

Arguments may blow up suddenly – you could probably sell tickets! – both tell it like it is without holding back. But if you bought a ticket, you'd have to get there quickly, because Orange-Orange arguments are resolved just as fast. There will not be any pent-up anger or lingering hurt feelings, and the next day neither partner may even remember what caused the fight. Get it out, get it on, and get it over with!

It's a good idea for Orange couples to hire others to take care of the routine and mundane in their lives. At work, there is likely someone Gold with strong organizational skills to manage the details, and at home, having a cleaning person is a treat since both partners like a clean and neat house, but prefer not to be the ones making it so.

Green and Green: The thinking couple

A Green-Green relationship is rare, as Green women make up only a tiny percentage of the population. When two do find each other (often on college or university campuses), they are happy to finally be with someone who truly understands them. These two have a relaxed and easygoing relationship, since deciding what or when to eat, what to wear, or which chores need to be done and when, aren't high priorities for either partner.

Both Greens love their independence and value being with someone who shares their need for space without pushing or nagging them. Their homes tend to be filled with high-tech gadgets along with the latest and greatest computers. Reading, or playing with the latest gadgets, are the perfect ways to spend their much-needed alone-time. Others may not understand it, but this couple is not above e-mailing or text messaging each other, even when they're both at home.

With their Green thirst for knowledge and lifelong love of learning, these partners love in-depth discussions and stimulating conversations. They motivate each other, supporting the drive for knowledge and understanding, while learning from each other. Within their small circle of friends and co-workers, this includes spirited exchanges with others who match their intellect, who might be experts in their fields, or who are knowledgeable about something of interest them.

To other Colors, it may seem that warmth and affection are missing in this relationship. While two Greens are not likely to hold hands, kiss in public, or show much emotion, every Green feels and cares just as deeply as any other Color – it's just that their public face is more reserved. It's impossible to judge the depth of a Green-Green relationship from the outside.

Blue and Blue: The feeling and caring couple

Blue men are as rare as Green women, so a Blue-Blue partnership is uncommon, but when it occurs, this special team tends to survive the test of time. Both partners are intuitively attuned to each other's needs, dreams, and emotions. The depth and total commitment to each other shows very clearly in this relationship, with a focus on taking care of each other and their many shared values. Building a strong and lasting bond just comes naturally to these two, who share an unwavering desire to make a difference in the lives of others.

For the Blue-Blue couple, few things are nicer than being able to escape the sometimes cruel world and go home to someone who truly understands their occasional roller coaster of emotions and strong intuition. It can be difficult when it's hard for both partners to say no and to set boundaries, but at least they both truly understand these challenges. It takes a lot for a Blue to exhibit any type of selfishness or confrontational behavior. During those rare times, it is important that their Blue partner is not also pulled down emotionally.

Neither partner requires or values control, or finds any need to engage in power struggles. Blue relationships are all about sharing, caring, being good listeners, and laughing and crying together. Both partners hold each other as their first priority and know they will always have a safe haven. For two Blues, their unconditional love is the tie that binds.

Relationship Hurdles

While each Color brings certain strengths to their relationships, there are also some relationship challenges specific to each Color. None of these challenges are intentional – they are simply natural manifestations of our Color personalities. But as any Green will tell you, knowledge is power, and we can never change or heal what we do not understand or acknowledge.

Blue Challenges

When Blues fall in love, they fall head over heels in love. It is unconditional, all-consuming, and often without boundaries or limits. Their partners are fortunate to have such unqualified support and encouragement, but Blues must be careful that they don't always put their partner and relationship ahead of their own needs.

- *Look after yourself first. It may sound selfish, but it's not! You give, and keep giving, to everyone around you, yet you often have nothing left for yourself. As a result, you can feel run-down and worn out. In small and gentle ways, you must learn to set boundaries and to say no sometimes. You will feel healthier, and be better equipped to reach out to others, if you take some time for yourself. There is a wonderful sense of freedom that comes from taking care of yourself, and once you've experienced it, you will be able to take better care of others.*

- *Understand when an issue is not about you or your feelings. It's certainly easier said than done, since turning off your emotions is never possible. It's not possible to turn off your emotions, but is your first reaction to always make it about feelings which can cloud your judgment? Could you sometimes first make it about facts, and then about feelings?*

- *Your best is all you have. Feelings that you have not done enough, that somehow you could have done more, are never helpful. In each situation, and with each person, you give as much as you can. When you truly believe that, it will show*

in your demeanor, your self-confidence, and in the way you
feel about yourself. Trust and believe that when you do your
best, God does the rest.

For other Colors lucky enough to have a Blue partner, there is one other important thing to remember: The silent treatment is one of the biggest Blue relationship killers. Not speaking, walking out or going away may seem like a good idea at the time, but it will have terrible repercussions. The silent treatment makes things worse, much worse, for our Blue loved ones.

Take half an hour to cool down, feel the frustration, stomp your feet and walk around the block. Then it's time to focus on healing and resolving the conflict. Take your Blue partner's hands, sit across from them, make eye contact, and speak openly and honestly. Do not let go of their hands until the issue has been resolved. For Blues, absence does not make the heart grow fonder – it makes things worse. Time does not heal all wounds – it only builds scar tissue. And not talking about the issue will bring neither forgiveness, nor healing, nor resolution.

Gold Challenges

Golds take their relationships very seriously and are loyal friends and fully-committed partners. But while they never take their relationships for granted, it can sometimes seem that way; Golds tend to focus on the tasks at hand, seemingly at the expense of their partners, who complain that their Golds had more flexibility when they were dating, and didn't care about what there was "to do."

- *Put aside your agenda more often. Sometimes it's okay to just go with the flow. When your partner has a change of heart, or wants to make different plans, honor them. Go along with their wishes and stay flexible. Who knows? If you keep an open mind – and an open schedule – it can strengthen your relationship.*

- *Understand that not everyone shares your need to be on time, every time. When others are relying on you, being on time is simply common courtesy. But does that always need to include being on time for a movie or concert? What's the worst that can happen if you're a little late? You might miss the coming attractions or ten minutes of the opening act. Making a big deal out of this little deal, pressuring and nagging your partner, creates stress and tension. Communicate honestly and openly about the specific times where being on time really does matter. Then be willing to compromise when late is not really late.*

- *Recognize that others see the world in shades of gray. To you, much of life is black-or-white, right-or-wrong. Know that this is not a perspective other Colors share. Be ready and willing to look at issues in your relationship through the eyes and the Colors of your partner. After all, wouldn't you rather be happy than right?*

Orange Challenges

Oranges add variety and excitement to any relationship. They are generous, action-oriented and eternal optimists, with a strong need for personal freedom. It is this latter quality which may make Oranges give up on a relationship when they start feeling tied down or controlled.

- *Not everything is fun. The rest of the world cannot change tacks as easily as you can. Your friends, co-workers, and partner may find it hard to keep up, or to realize when you have switched gears. It is particularly difficult for your partner, when they don't know if you're being serious or not.*

- *Fight fair. You have a strong competitive instinct and need to be a winner. Disagreements with your partner are not the times to make winning your primary goal. You can easily turn simple disagreements into arguments when you tune out with your favorite last word: "Whatever!" Is it really important that they lose and that you win? Will the end result not just be lose-lose anyway?*

- *Hang in there longer. Let's be honest, you like things fast and immediate. This can be an issue in your relationship. When things are not going well, you have a tendency to quit. Then there's that feeling that maybe there is something better out there. Think things through. Count to 100. Take your time before voting with your feet.*

Green Challenges

Greens' relationships may not always start on a romantic or emotional level. They value knowledge and intelligence and can first be attracted to someone who is able to mentally challenge them, and who has no need for a lot of external validation.

- *Speak from the heart. Yes, you find it difficult to talk about emotions, but it is important for many people. Share your feelings and allow your partner to see your emotions. It builds stronger bonds and will make for a better relationship, even though it may not seem logical. Besides, what's the worst that could happen when you trust your partner with your feelings?*

- *Calm, cool, and collected is difficult for others to understand*

and always appreciate. They do value your calm demeanor, but many times, your partner and others would rather experience your caring and gentle side. It strengthens your relationships when you trust someone enough to let them see the hidden side of you.

- *Share the meaning of Green alone-time with others. Let them know it is not optional, and that you need it. Rather than simply drifting away, explain to your partner what your needs are. This is your time to unwind and process your day. Your partner or others might wonder if you are angry or uninterested. It will be up to you to educate them about the value of alone-time because they may not understand or share the need for it.*

Fast Does Not Always Work

For many Oranges, acting or entertaining is the ideal career. As such, no exploration of Color relationships would be complete without a look at Hollywood.

One of Canada's better known exports, Pamela Anderson, married rocker Tommy Lee after having known him for four days, then filed for divorce within the year. In October 2007, Anderson married Rick Salomon during a short break between her Las Vegas shows. It was the third marriage for both of them. After two months, Anderson filed for divorce, but three days later she had the papers withdrawn while they attempted to reconcile. Within five months, all bets were off, and an annulment was granted.

Michelle Phillips, of The Mamas and The Papas, was married to actor Dennis Hopper for eight days. It was about quality for Phillips, not longevity. Nicolas Cage and Lisa Marie Presley easily surpassed the eight-day mark, staying together for three months.

Drew Barrymore's first marriage was to bar owner Jeremy Thomas whom she met six weeks earlier and decided to marry within a few hours. The marriage lasted five weeks, and was followed by Barrymore's two marriages (don't ask) to actor Tom Green, which lasted a year. That was followed by a "long-term" relationship to drummer Fabrizio Moretti. These days, insiders quote Barrymore as saying that she is not interested in another serious relationship.

Britney Spears is one of the most successful singers in the world, and her self-destructive behaviors have been well-documented. Her very public four-year relationship with Justin Timberlake was followed by a 5 a.m. marriage to childhood friend Jason Alexander, which lasted two days. Nine months later, Spears married Kevin Federline.

While we can't say which Colors these celebrities are, we know that Oranges value quick decision-making. Oranges have the potential to be successful at almost anything they choose. On stage or in front of the camera, they're usually winners. It is important to remember though, that in those situations, Oranges are in control and accountable only to themselves.

Making relationship decisions from that same mindset – thinking that they are solely accountable – poses a greater risk. Additionally, believing that they can be successful at anything can be a dangerous presumption. Prospering professionally takes very different skills than does building a strong, successful relationship. Divorce is forever, and in the Orange world, marriage and love are often measured more in weeks or months.

"Maybe God wants us to meet a few wrong people
before meeting the right one. So that when we
finally meet the right person, we will know

how to be grateful for that gift."
Author unknown

An ongoing study by psychologists at the University of Texas has been following 168 couples married since 1981. One of the findings in this study of relationships and the building blocks of successful marriages is the value of a slow and steady courtship. Slow and deliberate usually wins in a race against Hollywood-type romance.

How to Avoid an Intimate Relationship

A final thought comes from the *Saskatoon Pastoral Institute Newsletter*. It outlines ten steps to totally avoid an intimate relationship. It's sad, but true, each Color is amply represented:

Don't talk – if you are forced to talk stick to small talk and avoid discussing true feelings.

Never show your feelings – showing any emotions gives you away, thus they must be avoided.

Always be pleasant – especially if something's wrong – it's important to fool your partner.

Always win – don't compromise or it becomes a dangerous precedent to showing you care.

Always keep busy – it allows you to hide and send the clear message that work is more important than your relationship.

Always be right – among other things, it allows you to keep the upper hand and stay in control.

Never argue – or you might discover you are different, which would mean making allowances, adjustments, and compromises.

That could lead to letting your partner see who you really are, or know what you really feel.

Make your partner guess what you want – when they guess wrong, which they will often, you are able to tell them they really don't understand or love you.

Always look out for number one – after all, you are the one making all the sacrifices in the relationship.

Keep the TV on at all times – especially if you're talking. Best of all, nobody will even notice that you don't communicate.

Do you have any books on how to understand Gold parents or teachers?

I've been grounded so often, I taught myself how to play the guitar. Next week I start a 5 city tour — is that cool or what?

Chapter Eight

The Colors of Children: Doing More of What Works

Don't treat all your kids the same.
Treat them all fairly, but in the unique
ways which matter to their Colors.

Almost everyone who is blessed enough to have children of their own will remember a certain frustrated comment from their own parents: "Just wait until you have children of your own!" Now, here you are, and you finally understand what they meant!

Maybe their comment was followed by another: "I hope your children turn out just like you." That probably hasn't happened, as the odds of your children sharing your primary Color are low. And that makes this parenting business even harder and more confusing, since you can't call on your own childhood experiences, or the way your parents raised you, for answers.

It wouldn't be such a challenge if our children shared our personality type. We would have an idea of what to expect, an idea of when issues might arise. Two parents, each of different Colors, along with one or more children, each with their own personality types, makes for a very Colorful home. It also ensures that every parent will have at least one child whose behavior and reactions completely mystify them.

A common question from parents is whether someone's personality is predetermined at birth, or whether it is molded and changed over time and in reaction to life's experiences is a difficult one. Psychologists and behavior experts have valid opinions and much anecdotal evidence, but there is no broad agreement. Carl Jung, one of the foremost experts in the field, believed that we are born with our personality type in place, and that our families, the school system, and other external factors exert only marginal influence.

From the state of their rooms, to their learning styles, to communication preferences, children show their personality types pretty clearly and from a very early age. Clues to their Colors may be observed even in infants, where some seem to enjoy being left alone and never fuss much after waking up. Some babies thrive on physical touch and love being passed from person to person. Others are quiet and easygoing, while others still are already restless and always on the move.

When older children begin to think about "what I want to be when I grow up," their Color values influence their hopes and dreams. Money is rarely a factor in these early imagings. In fact, the majority of teenagers define success more in terms of being able to do something they love, rather than citing making money as their first priority.

Before she was eight years old, a family friend took singer Alanis Morissette to her first concert. It turned out to be a life-changing experience: it showed her that it was possible to make a living singing and entertaining. Long before she became a teenager, Morissette had notebooks full of original songs, had appeared on children's television shows, and had even recorded her first single.

Peer pressure, parenting styles, and a range of teachers, friends and experiences, make today's world something of a minefield for our children to navigate. Colors education provides children with simple and practical ways to express themselves. It helps puts words to their feelings and stressors, and gives them a greater understanding and appreciation of the Gold school structure. The insights of Colors also help children know that it is okay to be different from their friends, siblings, and parents. At home, children may subconsciously try to emulate the Colors of a parent, believing that they will be more loved, or somehow fit in better, if they are the same. This can cause real internal conflict when a child's own Color tendencies struggle against the behaviors they are attempting to emulate. In such instances, children may see the joys and strengths of their Colors as wrong, or signs of weaknesses. They may suppress the best parts of themselves in attempting to become something they are not.

For parents, these tools offer insight into the special qualities of our children. Understanding each person's Colors within a family eliminates the need to "mold" children to act – or react – in certain ways. Understanding why our children may have such different values and virtues – and challenges – reduces frustration and confusion, and brings us comfort in knowing that they will continue to grow into their own unique combination of Colors.

The most powerful A's your children want don't
come from the school system. They are your
approval, admiration, accolades,
applause, and attention.

Children need to know that their parents are 100 percent there for them. When you're at home, are you really there? Are you engaged? Are you mentally, spiritually, and physically available? Just as communication styles are different between adults, the same holds true for children. Conversations need to take place in the Color language of the child, not the parent.

Talking to your children without understanding the values and stressors of their Colors can create distance, fostering the feeling of a real generation gap. On the other hand, being attuned to their Colors can become a powerful tool for growing and strengthening your relationship and serves as a significant building block for their self-esteem. It also reduces frustrations and provides countless insights into the best ways to motivate and teach. For children, it is never the size of your paycheck, or the big problems of your work-world, but rather all the little things you do that impact their lives in powerful and lasting ways.

When you become aware of your child's Colors,
you are able to encourage and support them in
their dreams, instead of fitting them into yours.

Getting the Clues to Their Colors

I wanted to share my powerful story of what happened when I volunteered at my daughter's kindergarten one day. I had to get the children to sort, categorize, and graph boxes of Smarties. As we were doing the exercise, I noticed how differently they proceeded with their tasks. I immediately started looking at it through the eyes of Colors. Children are so pure at age five that it was easy to place them.

The Blues needed their hugs, a hand on their shoulder, as well as a little praise. The Oranges needed instructions with great excitement and enthusiasm. They couldn't sit still and wanted to get to the second page to see what was next before completing the first page. Of course, they were the first ones to ask when they could eat the Smarties. I was surprised that someone didn't do it without asking. Give them a few years, right?

The Greens got their instructions and totally ignored everyone else, zoning in on the task at hand. The Golds were very careful not to color outside the lines, concentrated quietly that each step was done in order and wanted feedback that they were on track and doing it properly.

The task went much quicker than expected and turned out to be a lot of fun for everyone. I had absolutely no frustrations, because I understood how to communicate with the kids in their Colors. The teacher was pretty amazed by how I was able to get all the kids connected to the task, and I just smiled. How sad that every teacher doesn't know these simple tools. This small but amazing experience made me see the world in a different way ... it certainly is Colorful and powerful.

C.G.

Until their mid-teens, the majority of children will exhibit many Orange behaviors, even if Orange is not their primary Color. A high energy level, trouble sitting still for long periods, and a need to test the rules and boundaries, are Orange behaviors all children share to some degree. Children are naturally curious, and experimenting, learning, and testing boundaries are an important and necessary part of childhood. Until children reach their mid-teens, there is no accurate test to determine the Colors of children. But it is not difficult to discover your own children's Colors by simply watching them at play, with their friends, when they're under stress, or while they're doing their homework. Even if you can't positively determine your child's primary Color, it is easy to see and hear what Color they are functioning in.

A Gold child, for example, is unlikely to skip school, as following the rules is already a strong, identifiable part of their personality, and the overriding guilt would not make it a fun day. Constantly looking over their shoulders, wondering when (not if) they will get caught, and already worrying about any repercussions makes playing by the rules much more attractive. It is their sense of responsibility, of knowing right from wrong, which is already a well-established part of their personalities.

Every Blue child loves to be hugged. For Blue children, physical touch makes them feel special and loved in ways words alone can not. Blue children are sensitive to the feelings of other children, and strongly value being part of a group, feeling helpful and included.

When a Green child says they'd like to leave class to visit the school library, they actually do! They are looking for some alone-time and they love learning, even at a very young age. As the father of a teenager who already holds a number of cancer research patents said, "I knew my son was different in grade seven when he didn't want to go play, but just wanted to read and do research."

Now if an Orange child asks to leave the class, teachers know that they would be well-advised to send someone along, just to make sure he or she actually returns to class. For Oranges, there is very much an early need for freedom, to leave the confined space of the classroom for a while.

This Family HAS To Understand Colors

I thought I'd write a note about my four children, each a different Color. So meet my family:

My Blue daughter is very involved with her church youth group, has a hard time saying no when asked to do something for them, to the point that she's a little taken advantage of, loves children, and just wants to be with them, and is especially helpful around the house. She feels the pain of her friends when they're having a hard time and just needs to be with them. She makes friends with her teachers and until she feels a friendship-type bond with them, she has a very hard time being comfortable in their classroom. She often reaches out to make friends or spend time with people who aren't the most outgoing.

My Green son had last years' Christmas list as a spreadsheet and the columns were labeled as most wanted, would be nice, good, and OK. In each column where the specific item was listed, he also included where it could be purchased and how much it cost, which he researched online. Then he went over the spreadsheet with me for a long time. He is planning his high school courses based on what majors he might want in college, which are based upon a solid, well-paying job that he'd enjoy. He likes to understand topics and subjects in great depth. When he was three years old he learned to ride a bike with no training wheels and practiced for days falling off, so he'd completely know how to control a fall so he wouldn't get hurt.

My Orange son wants to have fun and loves having a good time with people. Deadlines for a report? Oh, that's when you both start and complete it. He likes to play games and always did even when he was three years old he didn't care if he won or lost a game, he just wanted to play. He's very sweet and huggy a bit of blue shining through. When he was a baby we used to call him "Mr. Happy." He is considered gifted at school in the area of Language Arts.

My other daughter is so Gold, and so NOT Orange. She likes dependable schedules and to know what's going to happen and when. If I try to change the routine, it really throws her for a loop and can ruin her day. It can take a long *time for her to be comfortable with new people and each year before the first day of school, she wants to know what class she's in, needs to meet the teacher, be prepared in advance and even see where she's going to sit. She doesn't like change at all. She's VERY bright and wants to always get 100% on every assignment. She takes a long time to do her writing and has a very hard time making a "rough draft," because she wants it to be a final draft the first time she writes. She gets migraine headaches due to stress that she puts upon herself and can't understand why anyone would ever break a rule.*

My husband is Green and I am VERY Orange. It's a fun household with much respect and appreciation for each other, because of understanding our Colors.

N.A.W

You Can't Teach Them If You Can't Reach Them

Throughout the U.S., over 50 million children are enrolled in the school system. And each day, there are millions of incredibly gifted, committed, and talented teachers whose goals are to make a difference in the lives of children. Yet these teachers also face the realities of growing class sizes, shrinking resources, and staggering arrays of cultures, languages, special needs, and diversities. As a result, individual attention for each student becomes more and more difficult in a time when it is actually more and more critical.

If different Colors can be described as speaking the unique *language* of their personality type, their learning styles will also be different. However, that can become more of a challenge for school systems to incorporate. The basic teaching system in schools includes parts of each day, or certain classes, where students work independently with their own material and books. As a result, the classroom is expected to be quiet so that everyone can focus on their individual work. This template is the natural and preferred environment for most Gold and Green students. Large numbers of them tend to be introverts who measure and test their ideas against internal criteria in their minds, which is certainly easy for any school system to accommodate.

However, 70 percent of students are extroverts who do their best thinking with their mouths open. They need to verbalize their half-formed ideas and get others to react to them, since their primary focus is on the external world of things and people. Their ideal environment is one where they are able to verbalize what they are learning and to talk it through – to think out loud and to act out loud. It is how extroverted students tend to test their ideas, which is their yardstick of whether these ideas are worth retaining and adapting in the first place.

Building a model:	Greens and Oranges
Doing an interview:	Blues and Oranges
Going to the library:	Golds and Greens
Group discussions or debates:	Oranges and Greens
Homework through written reports:	Greens and Golds
Talking it through and brainstorming:	Blues and Oranges
Writing a journal:	Golds and Blues

For most Blues and Oranges, reading skills and comprehension are learned in much the same way. Before ever attending school, parents quickly realize that these two Colors do not enjoy reading as a silent, or alone, activity. It needs to be a fun and social activity, or it can be a constant struggle to have Oranges or Blues read in the first place. But when they are able to read out loud, do it together, adapt a magazine story with relevance to them, or when they can read to younger kids or others who will listen to them, it becomes a fun and social transaction.

One large and growing group of students who are much more able to utilize their preferred learning styles are the approximately 2.4 million children who are homeschooled, according to the National Home Education Resource Institute. Their parents are not richer, nor better educated than an average teacher, but are certainly more able to individualize and shape content to the learning styles of their children. It is almost always the same curriculum, but it is now able to be tailor-made to the Colors of their children. It is no wonder, that from the early grades, to standardized high school tests, and averages for college admission tests, these students perform better and achieve higher marks throughout their educational journey. While homeschooling is not easy for these parents, it is always worth it.

Eager to discuss new ideas
Diagnose the many difficulties you may face
Understand the potential of everyone
Communicate with them in their Colors
Accept them as they are, for each one is unique
Trust in what they thrive on
Improve on knowledge and understanding
Overbearing you should never be
Nudging gently to promote personal best

D. Erickson (adapted and used with permission)

I know you're dreaming big, honey. But with this much yarn, how large is the cat you'd like to get from the animal shelter?

Blue Children

Blue children come hard-wired to help others. It shows in their caring, their compassion, and their sensitivity to the needs of others. They need to make a difference. Parents will notice the signs that their Blue child wears their heart on their sleeve and may easily get their feelings hurt.

In a new school or new neighborhood, Blue children will make friends quickly and easily. Their open demeanor, willingness to share, and gift for making others feel special, naturally attracts friends. At any age, Blues will be the peacemakers, smoothing things over whenever possible. Even when they're very young children, Blue feelings run very deep.

Teachers will hear from them when a classmate is sad, sick, or absent. They will ask if projects can be done together, if they can help their friends, if they can take their buddy to the nurse's office. They are often looking for positive reassurances that they are doing well.

This focus on always wanting to help is as natural to a Blue as their positive attitude, their smile at a stranger, and their ease in making new friends. A Blue child playing at a new playground for the first time will often have a new best friend within the hour. Blues know just the right things to say to connect with people, and they are able to make everyone feel special and included.

I was sitting in the conference center of a hotel recently. Down the long hallway came two girls about four or five years old. They were running ahead and skipping around. Right behind them was their mother, and bringing up the rear by a good hundred feet, was their grandmother. Almost at the end of the long hallway, one of the girls turned around and became aware of how far behind her grandmother was. She ran back to her, grabbed her hand, and said: "Come on, grandma." The grandmother responded by saying that she didn't have to come back to help her. "But I really like helping people, Grandma, especially you," was the little girl's response. Surely a huge sign of a Blue girl already practicing what she feels strongly about.

Blue children readily share their toys and possessions and are aware of the wants and needs of their friends. If a friend prefers to do something else, or has a strong opinion about something, they will readily agree to a change. It is not about getting their own way, but about being together, sharing, playing, and having fun with their friends. Having to make independent decisions can often upset Blues, worrying that others would rather do something else. They tend to prefer decisions made by consensus, over championing their own cause.

The challenges for Blue children are the same as the ones for Blue adults: saying no, setting boundaries, and standing up for themselves. They want to fit in, to be loved, and to feel included, and these wants are strong motivators for Blue children to meet the needs of others, often at their own expense. A fight with a friend is devastating to a sensitive Blue child, whose feelings are easily hurt. Standing up for oneself is a difficult skill for some to learn, but incredibly valuable. Learning to say "no," and understanding that it won't harm a relationship, or make them somehow unlovable, is another valuable and necessary lesson.

Blue children often do hear what others aren't saying –
and often what they can't say themselves.

These challenges may continue into their teenage years, in spite of their best efforts to hide them. Blues understand the need to say "no," but most often do not feel it is the right thing to do. Blues live their lives by their feelings, not by deciding what is rational or logical. Because of this, Blue children are the most likely to be susceptible to bullying and peer pressure. At the same time, parents may be very proud of their Blue children fighting for the underdog and helping others. Blue children, like Blue adults, are optimistic, constantly looking for the good in everyone and everything. But as parents know, there is a fine line between being helpful and being taken advantage of.

It may be difficult for Blue children to understand that negative feedback is not a personal attack. Their self-confidence must be bolstered in order for them to internalize this. Blue children confuse negativity and criticism with personal failure. A simple comment from one of their friends, or a teacher, can have devastating effects which may linger for a long time. When offering feedback that could be interpreted as negative, it is important to first find something positive to say before addressing any issues or disagreements. Only then will conversations result in honest sharing, rather than hurt feelings.

Blues – no matter their age – can not tell their heart what to think. But when their feelings are hurt, it is important to teach Blue children how to focus on the issues or conflicts in a different way. Asking what happened just before the event, what other meaning a comment could hold, or how their friend might have been feeling, will often help direct hurt feelings toward a truer understanding of the issue.

Throughout their lifetime, a Blue will personalize many conflicts. In spite of all the evidence to the contrary, they often believe everything is their fault, and if only they had done more, or done something differently …

When it comes to conflicts in class, or disagreements with their friends, it is the parents who bear the brunt of their Blue child's unhappiness. Worried about jeopardizing their relationships or not being popular, Blue children will seldom say anything negative to their friends or their teachers.

Even when it comes to something extremely troubling, most Blue children prefer to ignore the issue until it (hopefully) goes away. It is so important for them to learn how dangerous this behavior truly is, and how it often makes things worse instead of better. Blue children can and should learn how to find creative and equitable solutions to their problems, making their relationships healthier and happier.

Our Blue children's stories and sharing will always be about people, never about jobs or tasks. They enjoy expressing themselves, and live life as a never-ending, unfolding drama. Blue children are poetic, have vivid imaginations, and possess strong listening and communication skills.

Blue children are also very creative. From dreams and stories to crafts and handmade presents, they show their love for others by making or sharing something special and unique. Both as children and adults, everything Blues do has a little piece of their heart in it.

Blue boys have the most difficult time in school and with their friendships. As one of the smallest Color groups, they often spend years wondering why they feel so different. Blue boys are much less competitive than their other Color counterparts. They care more deeply, are more compassionate, and are significantly more feelings-oriented than other boys.

At home, parents who do not understand Colors often make things worse. "Don't cry," and "Don't be so sensitive," are frequent comments. Consequently, many Blue boys end up hiding behind their second Color. Like a game-face, Blue boys use their second Color traits to hide their sensitivities and emotions until they feel it is safe to let others see them for who they really are.

Blue children value:
- harmony and getting along
- reading, if they settle down long enough
- open-ended instructions and questions
- the people-aspect of what they're learning
- agreement with others and getting along
- tact over truth
- feelings over logic
- daydreaming
- help with conflict resolution
- a sharing and caring environment

- lots of hugs
- pets (someone to love and take care of)
- helping others
- finding the good in everyone
- really being listened to and heard
- being happy over being right

> *"I would travel to every country in the world*
> *and tell people to love each other."*
> Sixth grade students' answer to: "What would
> you give the world as a Christmas present?"

Blue Learning Styles

Blue children love to start their days with a hug. At school, they thrive when learning is done in group settings and through team activities. They most enjoy school when learning is a group effort, involving frequent opportunities to share and interact with others. This working together and sharing with others builds Blue self-esteem and enhances both their abilities and their enjoyment. Strict deadlines help them stay on task, as does the possibility of being separated from their group should they not meet them. Blue children enjoy contributing and helping others, and they love the chance to be helpful to their team, their teacher, and their friends.

School is first and foremost about their relationships. Blue children have a strong need to feel included, and to be accepted and liked, both by their teachers and by their friends. Blues will be the first to notice when someone is not feeling well, is distant, or looking sad. The Blue radar is focused much more on school friends, rather than on school work.

Blues favor a group environment and cooperative learning situations where lessons are adapted to individual needs. They seek to make everything a team journey, involving frequent sharing and talking with others. Blues are not interested in processes or procedures; they are interested in their friends and the people around them. Stories, interactive games, and sensory-oriented activities are the easiest ways for young Blues to learn. They excel at social studies, music, and drama.

Blue children must understand the whole concept before they are able to deal with specific tasks or segments. Learning without an overview or outline can be a challenge, and Blues may be easily sidetracked, or start to daydream.

More so than any other Color, Blues thrive with same-Color teachers and instructors. Blue teachers are naturally attuned to the needs and desires of their Blue pupils, sharing their softer personalities and learning styles. Fortunately, the majority of elementary school, preschool, and daycare teachers tend to be Blue.

At school, it is up to the parents to communicate valuable feedback to teachers. Blue children are not likely to make their needs known, nor do they readily acknowledge when their feelings have been hurt. Every criticism hits them very hard and is taken personally. "You didn't do very well on this assignment," may seem harmless to a teacher, but your Blue child may have translated this as "You failed, and I don't like you anymore." It is vital that Blue children begin this lifelong journey of learning truly believing that a teacher's criticism is almost never a personal attack, but concerned, rational feedback meant to help them improve.

Only at home, with their parents, will Blues sometimes be honest and direct when their feelings are hurt. An awareness of this specific challenge is helpful for teachers, so they may watch that their Blue students do not succumb to peer pressure, or go along in order to get along. Teachers need to constantly watch that their Blue students have a chance to develop and voice their own opinions without feeling judged, or fear being laughed at.

Blue children appreciate:

- warm and caring instructors
- conversation
- learning from those attuned to individual needs
- group work and discussions
- the chance to discuss the human aspect of a subject
- frequent positive verbal feedback
- active listening from peers and instructors
- an easy-going style
- positive gestures, smiles, and reassurances
- safe and trusting environments
- being offered choices instead of demands
- no put-downs, judgments, or intolerance
- storytelling and sharing time
- being aware of the relationship dynamics in the group
- chances to help and contribute
- reasonable timelines and deadlines
- opportunities to build friendships
- when everyone is heard and their input is included
- "time off" to spend with their friends

What's family planning, Mom? I'm the only Gold in our family so I should probably be in charge of that.

Gold Children

Gold children may already be on the lookout for anything out of place, or not put away properly, by age two or three. Even this early, Gold children value neatness and tidiness much more than other Colors. The feelings of comfort and satisfaction which come when everything is where it is supposed to be, and the world is organized and planned out, are ones a Gold child will pursue throughout their lifetime.

It is one of the reasons why Gold children prefer to have their own rooms, or at least their own closets, or separate personal spaces, somewhere in the house. It allows them to organize their things in their own way, providing a sense of structure and order. This builds their self-esteem and helps them to relax. Unfortunately, a sense of structure and order is not important to their other-Color brothers and sisters, and this often causes needless stress and conflict – especially when they're sharing a room!

I'm a high Orange married to a Green, and our baby, who is three, is definitely Gold. This has been pretty prominent for quite a while – it just took learning about Colors to figure it out. Every toy in his room has a place, he keeps a few toys on show (which don't get touched until he changes them), his desk is empty unless he's using it, and my son has a schedule for himself that doesn't change.

The other day my son and his cousin were playing in his room – they usually play in his brother's room. It's OK to mess up his room: We get to play AND my room stays neat! When it was time to leave, I didn't check to see if the kids needed to clean up. Usually they don't make a big mess so I wasn't worried. We got into the truck and my son started in on me that my truck was "filthy" (his word). So to make him happy, we went through the car wash. (As a result, I forgot about half the things on my Orange sort-of to-do list.)

That night, I walked into his room, and it was as messy as his brother's! Every toy, book, and crayon was on the floor. I told my son he'd have to clean it in the morning, as I cleared a path to his bed. About 20 minutes later we heard noises from his room – which isn't like him to play after the lights go out. My husband put him back to bed, but this happened about three times before he actually went to sleep.

The next morning when I went into his room, it was spotless. Everything was back in its place! A little while later my son came to me and told me that he was sorry he wasn't sleeping last night, but it "bugged him" that his room was messy. He just couldn't sleep without cleaning up first. This happens at school also. The one activity for his playschool the other day was to cut out a paper star. Everyone in his class cut the paper *into a million little pieces and went on to something else. His actually looked like a star – but he was still upset that he went off the lines. When he colors, it's the same thing!*

Of course, we don't mess with his schedule too much, if we can avoid it. Before the last school break my husband volunteered to take the boys to school. Well I guess Daddy didn't do things "'right'," because his whole day was a little off, and after that he was still quite agitated when I picked him up. Since the Colors seminar we definitely parent differently. The kids have different punishments now, and the way we interact with them has grown a lot!

M.W.

Having their own rooms, desks, or separate play areas makes Gold children more comfortable and relaxed and helps them to study, read, and play better. A place in the house where they can organize their things, and where nobody "messes with their stuff," will become their oasis, perfect for doing homework or reading. Their Blue and Orange brothers and sisters may love to do their homework in the kitchen or dining room, but that doesn't work for Gold or Green children who need a quiet place to be alone.

Having their own space means Gold children won't have to spend time getting set up and organized before beginning their homework. Being allowed to choose their school supplies, letting them select just the right type of binder (yes, there are right ones and wrong ones!), organizer, and other items will make Gold children even more comfortable. It is an inexpensive investment, providing Gold students with a sense of satisfaction, knowing that everything is just the way it should be, and they are able to study properly, in peace.

It does not take long for Gold children to develop their strong sense of responsibility and concrete ideas of right and wrong. In their early teens, Golds may seem more mature than their other-Colored peers, and they may be more disciplined, getting their homework done before they play or relax. Often these Gold teens are very savvy about money, with large and ever-growing savings accounts. They think and plan carefully before spending.

Gold children have a finely-developed sense of values and standards. These come with fixed beliefs and strongly held black-or-white, right-or-wrong views. They seek fairness above all else, and this is especially true in regards to their siblings. Any perceived difference in treatment will quickly build resentment. For Golds, "it's not fair," has a much deeper meaning than for other Colors.

Golds tend to be quite patient and accepting of details and routines, and are very hardworking. Gold children are responsible and willing to help out when asked. All they require are clear and specific instructions and fixed responsibilities: "Tell me exactly what you want me to do, then leave me alone to do it."

Golds crave stability, the safety of fixed routines, and discipline which is fair and consistent. They build self-esteem (and their allowances!) by being helpful around the house. They don't need a lot of reminders, and will seldom use "I forgot" as an excuse. Gold children thrive on set rules and fixed boundaries. They feel safe and secure when they know exactly what is right and what is wrong. While it's not unheard of for a Gold child to skip a class or two, their feelings of guilt, and their worry about being caught and punished, together with their knowing that they are doing something wrong, generally make it a rare event.

*The police in a small town in Florida actually received
a phone call from a seven-year-old wanting to report
that he caught his grandfather cheating at cards.*

"What did I forget?" "Did I do a good job?" "What will my grade be?" "I'm sure I failed." "If only I had …" Many behaviors stem from Gold children's constant worry and concern. It can be greatly beneficial for them to be in a loving and understanding environment where they are able to verbalize these feelings. Talking it through with someone who can acknowledge the importance of their feelings lets Gold children begin to learn and believe that ninety percent of their worries are unfounded, and that their best efforts are good enough.

More importantly, they will learn that there are others who love them unconditionally, and value them for who they are, much more than for what they do. That they are loved for being good, instead of doing good, is one of the most powerful lessons for Golds to learn, and one that will pay dividends for a lifetime.

When it comes to playing with friends, or working with a group, Gold children are happy and comfortable in the background, behind the scenes, exerting a quiet influence when something needs to get done or be decided.

Gold children love to help others stay on task and organized, whether they're leading the group or helping as a teammate. When timing becomes important though, Golds are likely to step up and become actively involved in the group. Their team needs them, and they're happy to take charge and assume responsibility.

Without this timing though, group work can be a challenge for Gold children. They have very high standards, and prefer to work to these alone, without interference. It can also be hard to get Golds to commit to a group project. Once they are committed however, they will be fully involved and will do their best no matter what. Few things will distract them from seeing the project through to conclusion.

Gold children value:

- order and structure
- listening and learning
- clearly defined goals, objectives, and tasks
- practical over theoretical
- routines, consistent effort, and steady progress
- doing things their (the right) way
- an organized home and environment
- stability, predictability, and consistency
- a sense of belonging
- others who share the drive to stay focused
- positive reinforcement and encouraging feedback
- a close circle of friends
- following the rules
- doing the right things the right way
- being right more than being happy

Gold Learning Styles

Gold children look for structure and fixed routines, including in the school environment. Luckily, most schools are structured just this way. Set timelines, fixed rules, firm deadlines, and an emphasis on organization are all things Golds naturally value. When these elements are not in place, Golds will try to create them, since this will make them feel comfortable and in control and allow them to stay focused.

Gold children look for fixed systems, along with clear and detailed agendas. They value their own ability to stay on task and are upset when others get sidetracked, joke around, or roam off-topic. A big stressor for Gold students is a lack of clear instructions and expectations and a specific timeline. They crave fair and reasonable leadership and must clearly understand the criteria by which they will be graded and evaluated.

Golds want a lesson plan or agenda with distinct steps to complete in order to finish the task, and value grades and report cards as feedback to measure their progress. These are the students who ask if something will count towards their grade. Knowing something "will count" matters a lot – they want the tangible feedback of a graded assignment or test, but they feel the worry and stress that comes from needing to do well.

Golds prefer handouts, books, and materials which are readily available and which they do not have to share. They have the same high expectations of their teachers as they do of themselves. Golds are much more self-critical and much more concerned about their grades than other Colors. Gold children need to get the job done, and done right, before they can allow themselves to have fun and relax. They have a business-like approach to learning, but it is critical that Gold children learn that good enough sometimes really is good enough, and that it is also okay to have fun along the way.

My very organized fourth grade daughter's homework comes home every Monday and is due back Friday morning. When this started, I was "helping" her organize what she would do each day by labeling tasks with color coded Post-It notes. Being rather Orange, I had her do a little vocabulary work, a little math, then a little reading each day throughout the week, because this variety and changing things up seemed more fun to me.

We seemed to spend hours doing homework and at least once a week we both had stressed-out tears, and I was often at a loss of how to be more helpful. It was dreadful, to put it mildly!

About a week after I got home from my first Colors seminar, she asked if she could color code what she wanted to do each day. I was looking for anything that would help and readily agreed. I was surprised to see her color code her homework completely differently than I had been doing.

She chose one subject to do from start to finish each day. So, Monday was math, Tuesday was vocabulary, etc. The even more amazing thing is that she gets her homework done in a small fraction of the time it used to take, and with very little stress! All I could think about was, wow, Orange mommy, Gold kid! Thank you so much for opening my eyes to her Colors and how I can best respect when to step in and, more difficult for me, when to let her do her thing.

S.W.

Golds need lesson plans and tasks based on logical, step-by-step progressions. They need all the books and resource materials they can get. They thrive in band and in language arts classes, as well as in those subjects that have right-or-wrong answers, such as math.

Gold children have great focus, and they prefer to really master something and then readily apply it, rather than simply learning the basics of something and quickly moving on. Too much non-essential information, tangents, or even jokes and anecdotes, significantly detracts from their learning experiences. Some fun and spontaneity is okay, but only if they know the structure will remain intact, or that it's actually a scheduled component. Gold children try very hard to follow the rules – it's no wonder that most can claim the title of Teacher's Pet. Students who sit still, pay attention, and do their homework without being prompted? What teacher wouldn't appreciate that?

Gold children appreciate:

- working with timelines and schedules
- establishing and following fixed routines and formats
- high expectations for both their behavior and academic accomplishments
- an organized and structured environment
- quiet time to focus and get the task done right
- recognition for individual achievements
- clearly defined expectations, goals, and assignments
- concrete and specific steps to follow
- minimal group work
- measurable feedback and rewards
- logical reasons and rationale
- traditional teaching methods
- obedience, conformity, and accountability
- clear goal-setting
- access to available resources
- being motivated to do well – for themselves and others
- clear, fair, and well-known standards and rules

Remember when I said we should make the living room more fun?
When you went out you did say whatever!

Orange Children

Parents and teachers, fasten your seat belts, here come the Orange children! All children sometimes seem to have endless amounts of energy, but you can double that with Orange children. And no, it's not just a phase! They're not going to grow out of their frequent lack of attention to details, nor their high energy, rule-bending, short-cutting, multi-tasking tendencies. (They will be able to lower the volume though, as they get older.) Take comfort in the fact that these inclinations can be channeled in positive directions. Their "no fear" attitude and great people skills make it likely that they will be successful in any career which utilizes these traits. That doesn't mean though, that Orange children will not be a challenge.

The strong Orange personality may become apparent in daycare or preschool, creating some challenges for teachers – as it continues to do for parents. Even as infants, it's easy to see and sense the Orange restlessness and energy. They want out of their cribs and playpens and swings and chairs! They want to explore everything!

All the time! Restricting their freedom doesn't work, just like attempting to take away their freedom in later years doesn't work. Getting into trouble doesn't bother them – they simply learn to ignore it, believing always that there is no real harm done. Checking things out, trying something new, and pushing the envelope are tendencies which start early and will last a lifetime. After only a couple of minutes alone, Orange children can get into some kind of mischief. Oranges – no matter their age – do not handle boredom or solitude very well.

Orange kids are sociable, cheerful, bouncy, and popular. They seem to be magnets for other people, and they have fun and enjoy the social in life – for life. They collect many friends and take pleasure in being the star and center of attention wherever they go. From their first visit to the playground, Oranges are the leaders amongst their friends. They are consummate performers, thriving on attention and action, which greatly enhances their self-esteem. They make friends easily, love physical activities, hate to lose, and almost always have a bedroom that looks like it was hit by a tornado.

In their teenage years, being the star means looking good and wearing the latest and greatest fashions. It can make back-to-school shopping very expensive! An Orange "must" is looking cool and staying high on the "notice me" scale. If that requires a summer job and saving up, so be it. Even though planning and saving is an Orange challenge, saving money for clothes and other cool stuff is worth it. There won't be any money leftover for savings, but tomorrow will always take care of itself, and a week from now is an eternity away.

For Oranges, any attention is good attention. They want to be in charge and do things that are fun, without worrying about structure and planning. If planning becomes too complicated, or if others take over with a lot of rules and instructions, Orange children will quickly lose interest and move on. Unfortunately, they don't always mind if the attention is positive – negative attention is still attention. Being the class clown, rule-breaking, or just trying to press their parents' and teachers' buttons – it doesn't matter as long as they get noticed. It is best to downplay their negative behaviors and accentuate the positive ones, however minor. This is the best way for Orange children to learn that positive behaviors come with a much better payoff.

> *No, eight years old is NOT "almost a teenager." No, you can't "date" an alien. And will someone please tell me why a helium balloon is tied to the dog?*
>
> P.J.G.

An almost-daily exchange with her Orange daughter.

Oranges tend to have an "it's all about me" kind of attitude. They believe in squeezing as much fun out of each day as possible, with little thought of the future. "Is it practical?" "Is it fun?" and "Can I use this right now?" are three questions they consider before committing to anything. They do not want to be punished for attempts. Their creativity, and their tendency to think faster than they can speak, running ideas by the rest of the world, often has them talking things through off the top of their head. But they never want to be seen as ignorant, so they may adopt the attitude that something they are unfamiliar with is simply not worth learning, knowing, or doing. It makes them a winner in their own eyes, since they've opted out, rather than failed.

Too much structure, too many fixed routines, and too many rules to follow are big turnoffs for Orange children. No wonder they are often misjudged and misunderstood. It is also a reason why the number of children diagnosed with Attention Deficit/Hyperactivity

Disorder (ADHD) has grown over the past few years. Today, the U.S. Food and Drug Administration estimates that more than 2.5 million children take stimulant medication for ADHD.

It does not take much imagination to guess that the vast majority of these kids are Orange. And, boys are diagnosed with ADHD three times more than girls. As discussed in the Orange chapter, it is not a question of the legitimacy of ADHD, but it does warrant asking if sometimes drugs may be attempting to medicate a personality type. Labels last a lifetime, and quick fixes can sometimes do more harm than good. In fact, the American Heart Association has now begun calling for heart testing prior to prescribing any ADHD medication due to possible side effects concerning heart rates and blood pressure.

Over the past few years, more and more studies have also investigated the possible links between antidepressant drugs and violent behavior. In the words of author Mike Adams, who has reported extensively that many of these drugs have never been tested on children, nor approved by the FDA for use with children, "If you're going to alter the brain chemistry of these children you had better be prepared for the results." It is precisely why the United Kingdom has instituted a total ban on these medications for children.

More and more stories over the past few years have focused on the drugging of kids. Often, even from medical professionals, the question is asked why the initial action can often be the thought that one pill can be an instant solution. That is certainly the focus of many drug maker's advertising campaigns, that it's just that easy. However, the first responsibility is the parent's in focusing on improving their *child's diet, doing away with significant amounts of junk food, and eliminating almost all sugar-loaded soft drinks. Without minimizing the seriousness of a valid diagnosis, psychologists agree that there are many other avenues to try before considering medication. One of the most effective is a yoga class, as well as dance, art, or music. In addition, a serious focus should be placed on drastically reducing the child's sugar intake.*

Orange children value:

- immediate feedback and results
- knowing the practical reasons for doing something
- clearly defined, short-term goals
- imagination over observation
- curiosity – asking and trying anything
- challenges and dares
- being stimulated and entertained
- a what's the worst that can happen attitude
- the ability to wing it and negotiate anything
- staying flexible and leaving their options open
- multi-tasking
- hands-on activities
- any type of sport, game, or physical activity
- today's actions versus tomorrow's planning

Orange Learning Styles

From the corporate world to the school system, Oranges are usually misunderstood when it comes to the ways in which they learn, study, and retain information. Golds make up the largest Color group, and while they need quiet spaces in which to work and study alone (as do Greens), Oranges prefer to learn in exactly the opposite way. This can be especially challenging when Gold parents monitor and dictate their Orange children's study habits. The more alone-time Orange children are given, the more they – and their education – will suffer.

Oranges have no problem studying with a television on or their iPod playing. Parents know their Orange children are personable and highly intelligent, yet their grades do not always reflect this. This often leads to a Color clash, with non-Orange parents telling their children the proper way to study. Instead of creating success this more often than not leads to conflict, rebellion, stress, falling grades, and rule-breaking behavior.

One of the most effective ways for Orange children to improve their performance or to learn new material, is to study with their friends. Orange children are very verbal and very social. They are performers who learn best in short bursts. They need the freedom to move around and the chance to talk through ideas. Working with friends turns everyday studying into a competitive, social interaction, and allows Oranges to use their particular skills.

Oranges are motivated to succeed when there is something tangible on the line, as long as they can see the finish line. Ask any highly successful group of Orange salespeople at what point they get serious about a one-year contest and without exception, they will admit it is in October or November, not in January at the start of the contest. Any parent who uses the reward method with their Orange child needs to make sure the reward pertains to today, or this week, and not the school year in its entirety. The end of the year is much too far away to generate any type of interest or motivation in a live-for-today Orange.

Since the Orange learning style is quite different than the Gold norm, typical instruction methods rarely work. Parents and teachers quickly discover that Orange children need to be entertained, and that they learn much better when activities are hands-on, participatory, and fun. Learning to sit still and concentrate on written work is a continual challenge for Orange students – and their teachers. Whether appropriate or not, if the fun is missing, Oranges will gladly provide it – anytime and anywhere.

Make it a game and give me a chance to win
and I won't quit on you.

Truly connecting with Orange children in a learning environment, and keeping them focused and interested, is a special challenge. Oranges excel when they can learn through hands-on activities and when there is a game or a contest involved. If they're bored, then watch out! Both positive and negative attention is fine – being the class clown is just as rewarding as being the class star.

Orange children excel when they've been given practical, clear instructions and expectations. They seek instantaneous, concise feedback and flourish with teachers who are flexible and innovative. Orange children routinely leave their assignments incomplete until the last minute. Written homework is the biggest challenge because it doesn't offer Oranges the chance to perform, to use their presentation skills, or to improvise as they go along. As a result, homework assignments may often not be indicative of their knowledge or understanding.

Kids, and especially Orange kids, fidget, and can't sit still. But a Minneapolis-St. Paul area teacher had an idea. Abby Brown wanted to do something way out of the box for her sixth grade class to address these continuous challenges. What if kids could stand during her classes, instead of sit? On her own initiative she has designed a stand-up desk for her classroom. It comes with a lever, just like office chairs, to adjust the stand-up desk to the height of each student.

The results have been amazing. The fidgeting has measurably decreased, her students can move around a bit, and are not nodding off or daydreaming. The quality of the class-work is up and grades are measurably improved with such a simple, yet powerful idea. The ability to move around is huge for kids of all Colors, and with less physical activities and sports in many school districts, these so-called "activity-permissive classrooms" may well be onto something.

Schools from California to North Carolina have begun using these desks, and many other school districts are making the trip to Brown's classroom to see for themselves. It may be worth observing or experimenting at home. Is there a kitchen counter with stools your Orange child can use? Can you buy an inexpensive or used drawing table? It will let you observe for yourself if your kids study better while standing up or sitting down. (Do keep in mind that the need of Gold and Green kids for a quiet area to study will still be their first priority).

Oranges much prefer the social parts of the school day – recess, dance, music, and drama – where they can both perform and learn something. These are also areas where they can best show off their creative skills and talents. Orange children look for varied instruction and concrete activities that teach practical material. They evaluate much of their learning in terms of "What's in it for me?" They seek immediate feedback and look for chances to be the star, the center of attention, or the winner, no matter the subject. Anything that can be made into a game or a challenge appeals to their competitive nature. While that may be possible in the workplace, it is more difficult to accommodate in a school setting.

Many school districts have now implemented policies preventing teachers from making grades public or recognizing individual students. While there may be valid reasons for these policies, Orange students suffer. When competition and public praise are removed from the classroom, Orange students more than any others lose their primary motivations to succeed. Unfortunately, difficulties in class can then lead to acting out, which leads to more discipline. This may result in Orange students mentally checking out or physically dropping out.

Oranges learn best, and learn quickly, through trial and error, through working things out and talking them though. Textbooks and theory make sense only after the hands-on effort, after they have experienced the how and the why first hand. "Let me at it," and "Let's see how this works" are their battle cries. The music business is full of incredibly talented Oranges who learned to play their first instrument in just that manner, with no formal musical training. It's all about *Just do it*, not, *Let's read about* and *learn the rules*.

One more point to ponder: Ask a few Orange colleagues, or church friends, how long they think any meeting should last. Most will agree the optimum length is twenty minutes. Now, think about how long a typical high school class lasts, or even how long Orange children are expected to sit still and do their homework ...

Orange children appreciate:

- hands-on activities
- visual and spatial intelligence
- experimental activities
- concrete activities to teach abstract ideas
- a variety of tasks
- the ability to stay active
- kinesthetic learning
- challenges and competitions
- the chance to win
- the opportunity to show off
- physical challenges
- minimal rules and lots of flexibility
- minimal emphasis on written material and reports
- a fast pace – keep it moving, keep it fresh
- experimentation and the chance to try without judgment
- frequent feedback – but not on experimenting
- games, races, built-in contests
- the freedom to complete something their way
- varied displays, changes of scenery, and frequent breaks

I know you're dreaming big, honey. But with this much yarn,
how large is the cat you'd like to get from the animal shelter?

Green Children

Parents, get ready! Green children become very independent, very quickly. It might seem as though there's a mini-lawyer in the house, since from a very early age, Green children ask a lot of probing questions and never settle for the easy answers. Detached and naturally curious, Green children are also easygoing and flexible – until something runs up against one of their principles or beliefs. Then they dig in and stand firm.

Green children ask questions. All children go through the "why?" stage, but with Greens, parents may feel like they're on the witness stand as their child asks deeper and more probing questions. And, once they've processed the answers – an hour or a day later – they may rephrase the question and ask for clarification. Or, they may have spent time researching and have follow-up questions.

If you don't know the answer, you'd better admit it, as Green children are masters at spotting inconsistencies and faulty reasoning.

And neither "because,"nor "I don't know," are acceptable. This thirst for knowledge is one that will continue throughout their lifetime, as will their never-ending need for understanding and intellectual growth.

Make me think! Don't just make me listen.

From the time they learn to read (or turn on a computer), Green children enjoy learning, puzzles, and figuring things out for themselves. They are perfectly content on their own, and they choose to have a very small circle of friends who share their joy in learning and exploring and who can challenge them mentally.

Green children enjoy the time and space to learn, explore, read, find answers, and problem solve. They are eager for mental stimulation and view problem solving in the same way their Orange friend does sports. For Green children, learning will forever be a hobby, not a chore.

Their well-thought-out positions and well-reasoned answers can make Green children appear strong-willed, confident, and persuasive. Greens have no problem standing alone against the world when they believe they are right. That's not to say they are inflexible – Greens are more than willing to change their opinions if they're shown, through logic and facts, the necessity of doing so. But neither authority nor emotion will ever come into it.

When Green children "get it," when the light goes on and a new concept or theory makes sense, their self-esteem grows. Greens of every age love being able to make all the pieces fit together. They are very excited by new ideas, new concepts, and meaty problems, all to be dissected, examined and solved in an objective and critical manner. Greens are seldom swayed by their emotions which they prefer not to show, even with their own family. Sharing any emotion or affection can have them feeling awkward and uncomfortable.

A Blue mom recently exchanged notes with her daughter at a seminar. She sent her a note with "I love you" written on it. But with a Green daughter, she shouldn't have been surprised when she got this note back: "Please don't say that in public. No one needs to know. Don't say it out loud, ever. We all just assume that we love each other and nobody has to say it out loud unless they're losers." Ouch!

Green children tend to be introverts, quite shy outside their immediate families and few close friends. They are not social creatures and usually prefer to work on their computers or read instead of attending social functions. They will likely ask why they have to come, why they can't stay home, even when it's a family outing. As parents, it's best to be prepared for these questions, and to know that if they do come, they'll probably bring something to read – just in case.

Green teenagers are much they same. They are perfectly comfortable spending time alone, and are not likely to be involved in team sports or group activities. They may participate in some, but it's not their preferred environment. On a positive note, it matters very little to them what other teens think. Greens are the least likely to succumb to peer pressure.

Logic and facts trump emotions and feelings for Greens. This makes it doubly important that Green children learn to understand the power emotions hold for others, and to recognize that what others feel is often just as important as what they think. Green children often do not understand how their words or comments may be hurtful to others.

Green children evaluate issues logically. Having your feelings hurt because of the outcome of that logic doesn't make sense to them. What they said wasn't meant as a personal attack. It wasn't even a criticism, really. How could sharing information and feedback, or pointing out a wrong answer, be hurtful? Green children's relationships will benefit when they learn the value in finding positive common ground.

Green children – and their parents – already know they're intelligent. So do most of the people with whom they interact. But their impatience with those less clever is often apparent by the look on their face and the frustration in their voice. ("I already told you!") There is huge value for Greens in understanding that there are times when others look to them for verbal reassurances, expressions of gratitude and appreciation, and that the connection formed when these reassurances are given helps build relationships. This is a lesson that will also serve them well as adults.

Green children may be labeled as "geeks" in high school, but they will always be popular when others need help or explanations. The challenge for Green children is to make those explanations and ideas simple for others to understand, without condescending.

Green children value:
- theory first, then application
- open-ended instructions
- written over oral
- reading and listening over participating
- challenges, research, and new horizons to explore
- space and independence
- being the strong and silent type
- independent work and learning
- thinking it through before doing it

- new problems to solve
- understanding the reasons behind new ideas
- truth over tactfulness
- few words but many thoughts
- credibility more than harmony
- knowing when they're right and fighting for it
- being in the know more than being happy

Green Learning Styles

Green students are quiet and intelligent. They focus on their studies and have little interest in extracurricular activities. Greens seek to really understand and internalize the concepts, principles, and specifics of what they're studying. They need time to think about points brought up in group discussions and the chance to dissect material in detail, often wandering off alone during breaks, finding a quiet place in which to process what they have learned, and to think through the material.

Green students typically do not feel comfortable in large groups or in noisy classrooms. They need time to process and absorb materials, and they thrive with teachers whose presentations are well-planned and logical, and which offer opportunities for discussion, debate and questions.

There aren't many questions Greens do not want to ponder – the more complex and intricate, the better. They thrive in investigatory and participatory learning environments. Greens love to play devil's advocate, keeping a good discussion going, and pulling out all points of view. When they find peers whom they believe are credible and able to challenge them, Green children are very much in their element.

Beginning at a very early age, Green children look for friends and work-partners whom they feel are credible. They look for teachers whom they can respect, and whose knowledge and in-depth understanding of their subject helps them take specific material and relate it to the big picture. Very early in life, and in all walks of life, Green children are in search of trustworthiness, reliability, knowledge, and honesty – in themselves and in others.

Recently a mother called, who was quite concerned about her Green daughter's math grades. In Grade 10, her final mark was a 95%. That was not a big surprise, as math tends to be one of Green's favorite subjects. Yet for the first half of her Grade 11 course, her daughter was barely passing. After just a few questions, it became clear that her daughter was convinced her math teacher "knows nothing about math."

While her mother did not want to think in those negative terms, her daughter had been sending a lot of signals that she could not get over the perceived lack of her teacher's credibility to focus on the course content. Without the maturity of an adult, or the tools of Colors, it was as though she wanted to prove the accuracy of her judgment. If she could simply study from home or in the library, her daughter would certainly get the same high marks at the end of the year while learning on her own. Even for teenagers, the Green need for credibility of others, and themselves, shows itself in many ways.

Green children enjoy independently researching material and thrive on sharing what they have learned with others. Their favorite subjects tend to include math, history, and science, or any areas involving complex problems which stimulate their minds.

... wondering about my eight-year-old who is trying to figure out how to make wireless electricity (because internet can be wireless) ... but refuses to learn his 4 times tables!

M.H.M.

Green children appreciate:

- group brainstorming, but individual reports and assignments
- many paths to the goal with milestones and deadlines marked
- real world problems
- clear, simple, and logical instructions related once
- sufficient research time
- built-in time for questioning and exploration of subjects
- links to future benefit and implications
- tie-in (fit) of material to what they already know
- credibility in material and instructors
- rewards for their research, skills, and interpretations
- lots of available resources, including computers
- time to process, research, mull, discuss, perfect
- a factual and logical focus
- the ability to contribute input, interpretation, and their ideas
- that best efforts are always given and required
- emphasis on outcomes, results, and implications
- juicy questions and stimulating discussions

Making a Difference

It takes talent, commitment and drive to be an effective teacher today. Our education system is struggling with rising expectations, budget cuts, and changes in the student population. Add in all our children's different needs and personality types, and it's hard to believe anyone is willing to pursue such a challenging career. Yet there are countless numbers of teachers who are constantly finding unique and creative ways to deal with the rainbow of colors in their classrooms.

By all accounts, Henry was one of the best teachers in his high school. He is Green/Gold. (Along with Gold/Green, this is the color combination of a large number of teachers.) His classes consisted of more than 50 percent Orange students whose mind-set toward rules, deadlines, and being on time was quite the opposite of Henry's. Even decades ago, he started to realize that traditional learning styles were not going to reach these kids.

Through trial and error, Henry addressed both those issues in practical and easy ways that made him one of the school's favorite teachers. By incorporating the use of tools and lots of hands-on exercises and projects, he gave these kids a chance to actively contribute in class.

An appropriate method of disciplining Orange students was always a challenge. The traditional method of sending them to the principal's office had minimal effects on his students. In fact, to many, it was almost a status symbol amongst their friends. It became more of a way of showing off, rather than one of effective punishment. Henry's Green/Gold personality also wanted to deal with this challenge himself without simply passing the problem off to administrators. This reflected his strong Gold sense of accepting responsibility and the strength of the Green mindset in looking at the big picture and finding an innovative solution.

But Henry needed to deal with the pent-up Orange energy of most of his students, their need to always be on the move, and their lack of proper school discipline. His solution was simple, yet powerful. "Get down and do 20 push-ups!" While his students were horrified at first, it soon became almost a game in his classes. It was an innovative solution which balanced the need for discipline with a very Orange chance to show off and do something physical.

To this day, Henry often runs into students who graduated decades ago. Some of them will still drop to the ground in the middle of a mall and excitedly show off to Henry, and now their kids, that they can still do the 20 push-ups. They were and are Orange, and although adults now, they still love to perform and show off to a teacher who made a difference.

Missing Male Elementary Teachers?

The start of every school year generally brings renewed media interest in the lack of male teachers at the elementary level. The majority of high school teachers are Gold, as are most school administrators. Greens tend to be college and university professors. Oranges aren't well-represented in the profession at any level, with the exception of subjects such as shop, drama and physical education – those "hands-on" subjects where "doing" is the norm.

Blues make up the largest Color group of teachers and staff in elementary schools, daycare centers, preschools, and kindergartens. Women make up more than 90% of all Blues. It makes sense then, that we're missing some male teachers.

According to surveys, men make up less than 16% of

elementary school teachers. Of course, success in school is not dependent on the gender of the teacher. A teacher's experience, commitment and passion, together with an understanding of Colors and their impact on learning style and behavior, can make a huge difference. It is disappointing though, that our children are missing that added dimension that would come from more Blue male teachers in the early grades.

The Parent-Child Combinations of Colors

The combination of Colors in a parent-and-child relationship makes for some challenging situations. When each person in the home has different values, needs, motivators and ways of communicating, there can be struggles.

Following are explanations and practical suggestions for finding some common ground. If you read them and think, "I knew that, because I do that," then, congratulations! The motivation behind some of your child's behaviors may not come as a surprise. But others might provide you with new answers and ideas about some old, nagging questions.

Parents learn many things from their children, and often these come from the natural strengths of their Colors. It is important to be mindful that every child's development, learning, and growth happens, at least occasionally, in all the Colors. And isn't that what we all want? What could be better than a child who can experience the positives of all four Colors? It expands their horizons, stretches their comfort zones, and strengthens all of their relationships.

Blue Child and Gold Parent

You'll need to moderate your practical approach and your task-and-procedure focus. Your Blue child is very expressive and very verbal. The stories they share are long and involved, with an emphasis on people and feelings. Their dreams do not always sound practical, but they should always be encouraged. Do help them bring their exaggerated problems down to size, and focus on teaching them practical solutions without giving them only black-or-white choices. Be mindful that Blue children will almost always try to avoid anything negative or unpleasant.

Teach them the skills they need to bring about closure, how to actually resolve something instead of ignoring it and making it worse. The Gold sense of duty is the Blue equivalent of helping people, so you both share a strong sense of belonging and feeling included when you volunteer – do so, together.

Blue Child and Orange Parent

A Blue child's feelings may be easily hurt by their Orange parent's bluntness, kidding around and teasing. They might not say anything, and likely they'll still be smiling, but it's up to the Orange parent to notice and take action. Blues are most sensitive when they feel their Orange parent is rushing them, or not really listening. Be patient, parents! Blue stories may be long, and it takes time to really hear what your child is saying – but it's worth it. Stop multi-tasking, and listen. You'll be showing your child that they're worthwhile, that they are the most important thing in your life.

Appreciate the fact that both you and your Blue child share strong Orange verbal skills and a love of acting and performing. An Orange parent's popularity with their large group of friends is equivalent to a Blue child's deep and meaningful connections with theirs. Show them that popularity is not always about giving in, and that standing up for their needs will not make them unlovable or unpopular.

Blue Child and Green Parent

Dealing with the deep, overriding, and ever-present emotions of Blue children can be a challenge. They worry what others think and often act accordingly. Share your Green skills, and show your Blue child that evaluating facts may be as helpful as understanding emotions in some situations. Teach them how to step away from their emotions when necessary and appropriate. Do be aware that often your Blue child may understand something, but until they feel it in their heart, nothing will change.

Blue children thrive on frequent verbal affirmations, reassurances, and lots of hugs. Listen to their long stories without a Green unexpressive look on your face, and practice interactive communication skills with them. You share strong verbal skills and the joys of fantasy.

Blue Child and Blue Parent

Your Blue child is so easy to feel close to. They share your craving for intimacy and physical touch, long after it's no longer "cool" for other Colors. You understand each other without needing words, and communicate the power of dreams, feelings, and living life within the heart. Empathy, the knowledge that feelings and hurts run deep, and the drive to help others will always connect you.

Blue parents value comfortable, loving, and safe homes, but will have trouble acting as disciplinarians. Try to keep some structure, and to have firm rules which can't be bent, no matter what. Remember that your Blue child will easily sense your mood, even when you try to hide it. They take on your feelings of hurt and pain, and are extraordinarily intuitive when it comes to emotions. Work these through together.

Green Child and Green Parent

Green parents and children share a joy in learning and an enthusiasm for discovery and research. Neither will settle for a "because" answer, and both understand there are logical consequences to all actions. Green parents should encourage their child's easy-going attitude, and encourage them to be accommodating when appropriate. Allowing them to grow into their natural lateral thinking skills, making sure that their alone-time doesn't become excessive, and showing them that snap-decisions are not always the right decisions, will help them grow into the best Green adults they can be. Just like their parents!

Green Child and Gold Parent

The Green and Gold challenge in your family may often come down to freedom versus structure. Your Green child may view the many "house rules" as illogical and confining. Flexibility and explanation will smooth things out. Green children need personal space and the ability to "opt out" of the occasional family outing. They enjoy their alone time, and can certainly be trusted with it, though it's common for them to lose track of time missing meals and skipping chores when they are single-mindedly focused on something new.

In the school years, your parent-child relationship grows even stronger, as your Green children excel in many subjects, sharing your belief in the importance of education. Learning, reading, and exploring are all great investments in their future. Don't be overly concerned about their fashion sense, or lack thereof. Most Green children – and Green adults – feel that what they wear is just not as important as what they think.

Green Child and Blue Parent

Your Green child's sharp mind and inquisitive nature will be apparent from day one – enjoy it! Be proud of their strong drive to find answers, and of their love of learning. It can be hard to always understand their need for independence, privacy and space, but their alone-time is necessary and important – and the need for it won't go away. Be careful not to smother them, or try to "cheer them up." They're not mad, or sad, or lonely, no matter if that's how you, a Blue, would feel in their same situation. They choose to have fewer friends and attend fewer social functions. There is no reason to feel sorry for them or to worry about them – it's the choice they've made.

Be mindful that even your open-ended questions will result in short, to-the-point answers from your Green child. It is nothing personal – it's just their nature. Work to show them that social interactions are valuable, and that they can be precious and important. Encourage them to expand their circle of friends when warranted, and to not judge others solely on intellect.

Green Child and Orange Parent

Your Green child is all about learning and thinking. Wait, not hanging out with friends and having fun? It may be hard for an Orange parent to understand, but your child thinks that is fun! And luckily, your Green can be trusted to handle the responsibilities of freedom. Do remember that most tend to be introverts, so help them expand their social skills, and pull them out of their comfort zone occasionally – and away from books and computers.

As an Orange parent, you can help your Green child understand the benefits of small talk, and to become more comfortable in social situations. Share with them how to be flexible and that it's okay when someone doesn't have the answer. Show them traditional ways to have fun and why it's important to do so. They might never be as comfortable in the world as you, but there is much for them to enjoy and discover. And know that sometimes they just need to stay home (and that that's fun too).

Orange Child and Orange Parent

It is always playtime for you two! You don't take anything too seriously, and if something goes wrong, well, your Orange child will learn their lesson and move on without too many consequences. Your arguments can be loud and frantic, but there's never any hard feelings or lingering resentment. Be careful of both your winning-is-everything attitudes and share with your child some of the painful life-lessons you've learned.

Orange children are involved in sports, and Orange parents are the loudest cheerleaders. Remember your own childhood experiences – what you needed more or less of – and use them when you parent your Orange child. Those lessons may help in teaching how to slow down, and why it's not necessary to always push the envelope, find a shortcut, or bend the rules. Help your child channel their creativity and their positive attitude and focus on completion. You might learn something yourself!

Orange Child and Green Parent

Your Orange child's energy can be a little worrying, right Green parents? It's hard to keep up with them, and it sometimes feels like you're living with – and in – a hurricane! Help your Orange child to see the long-term; help them to understand that instant gratification isn't always the answer. It won't be easy!

Be careful that your response to your Orange child's need for immediate, short and quick answers does not have you automatically saying no every time. Show them that there are times when it is best to think first because everything has consequences. You'll help your child avoid a lot of pain and trouble if you're able to teach them the skills to slow down and think before pulling the trigger. Remember that you share both a pragmatic world view and a sharp tongue – just try not to use them on each other!

Orange Child and Gold Parent

Luckily, you're not in for much conflict here, at least not in the early years. Any trouble will most likely be the result of your Orange child's high energy level and the fact that they're into anything and everything. Do buy them quality, durable toys and clothes if you can, as they are very hard on both. The fewer rules the better for your young child, who needs the freedom to play and have fun. Later, your Orange teen will constantly challenge your Gold authority, rules, and structure. They feel any discipline is unwarranted, and often rebel. The more rules you lay down, the more they tend to fight them.

Try to get your teen to voluntarily buy into a smaller number of fixed rules. Could there be a half-hour curfew leeway at times, or an easing up about the state of their room? Setting rules about certain clothes or hair color are a waste of time, as these decisions are made on the spur of the moment with their friends, not pre-planned with the intention of breaking the rules. Teaching your Orange child to understand the value in seeing something all the way through to conclusion will be a valuable lesson. And their realization that a little focus can have a big payoff will serve you both well.

Orange Child and Blue Parent

Your Orange child's creativity and adaptability is something to be celebrated. Be proud of their "people-first" attitude, their large circle of friends and their strong verbal skills. You probably do feel some concern about your Orange child's tendency to speak their mind, often unintentionally hurting feelings. It's up to you, as the Blue parent, to teach them by pointing out the consequences of their *speak first, think later* actions.

Life with an Orange child is never boring. They often exaggerate and embellish. And while they are generous to a fault, Oranges definitely have a strong stubborn streak and absolutely no hesitation about standing up for themselves. This can be worrying, especially when you're imagining your child's future. Too, you have your own Blue challenges in setting rules and following through with discipline. While Orange children certainly need fixed boundaries and a firm hand, it is difficult for a parent with such a loving heart. Work together and your relationship will flourish.

Gold Child and Gold Parent

Your Gold child follows the rules, earns their allowance, and helps around the house. They need minimal reminding or supervision. Sound familiar? Gold parents often think, "She's just like me!" Your challenge is not to pass on your worry over details, so no rattling off, "Did you remember to ..." and, "Or what about ..." Be vigilant that your Gold child is not missing out by spending time too much time emulating your planning and structure. A carefree attitude is an important and essential part of childhood.

Make sure that having fun is always on both your to-do lists. Share your own experiences and teach your Gold child not to take everything seriously. Let them know that it's okay when their perfect plans need to allow for some flexibility. And remind them of the most important lesson you've learned over the years – that what they worry about rarely comes to pass, and if it does, you can handle it together.

Gold Child and Green Parent

Your Gold child just wants to get on with things! It doesn't matter if they have to redo some part of it, they just need to finish it. This can be difficult for a Green parent to understand, but Gold children need closure – now! You will teach your Gold a valuable lesson if you can show them the benefits of doing it right the first time, and the value in thinking things through and doing them properly, rather than just getting them done (and crossed off the list).

Gold children always ask the "how" questions. Parents should try to show the value of the Green "why" questions too. Teach your Gold child that while it's important to have a plan, it's just as important to know how to implement that plan. It may be a challenge for a Green parent to give their Gold child firm directions, unbending rules, and enforced boundaries, but it's necessary for both of you. While you may wonder why your child is always looking for the black-or-white solution rather than thinking things through, you can help them develop lateral thinking skills that will benefit them in the years to come.

Gold Child and Blue Parent

Your biggest challenge here will be providing the firm and fixed rules that your Gold child craves. Structure and stability make your Gold feel safe and protected. Blue parents have a hard time enforcing discipline and strictly sticking to the rules, and your Gold child knows this and may use this against you when they want to press an issue.

Golds don't ask for rules, but discipline and routines structure their world. Blue and Gold share a desire to help others and do their best, but they have different motivations. The Blue parent wants to be helpful – needs to be helpful – while the Gold child views it as their duty. Your Gold may have few friends, but don't worry – it's quality, not quantity that counts, and your child knows this.

Finally, don't worry if your child doesn't readily share stories. Golds generally focus primarily on relaying factual information. Remember though, it doesn't matter what they share as long as they're sharing it with you.

Gold Child and Orange Parent

Your Gold child easily adapts to structure and routine, but it's your job to show them that life is a great adventure. There is a big world to explore, filled with great experiences to expand their horizons. Point out the positives whenever they venture from their set patterns and fixed schedules.

Orange parents, give the setting of boundaries and enforcment of rules your best effort! They are necessary – at least in part – for your child. Your Gold child may worry and plan much more than you, so always try to show that having fun and relaxing are important parts of life. Your Gold will be better behaved and less active than you were at their age, so take pride in the fact that they are doing well in school, and that written work comes easily. Remember that keeping your word and sticking to agreed upon plans is critical for your relationship – if it's on their to-do list, it's important!

So Tell Me What Happened at School Today?

Even for children, their communication styles will revolve around their primary Colors. They will share stories and information in the language of their Colors. They may be the same set of circumstances, but will be told quite differently.

Gold: "I got an 89 in math and then Mrs. Jackson wasted 15 minutes while they were trying to collect everyone's 20 bucks for the field trip next week. Plus, I have an assignment that we have to do by next Friday, so I'm going to my room to do homework."

Blue: "Today I told Mrs. Jackson that she's my favorite teacher and then I got to help her. We were collecting the $20 for the field trip next week and she let me help. My friend Linda wasn't feeling well before lunch, but Mrs. Jackson wouldn't let me take her to the nurse's office when I wanted to go with her to make sure she was OK. But she's fine now cause I shared my lunch with her. Can I call her to come over after supper? Please?"

Orange: "Ahhhh! My friend Karen, like, you know the one that got me grounded for no reason – like it's my fault she didn't have her watch – well, like, she bought the coolest jeans, I gotta get a pair like that so we're gonna go to the mall after supper because I don't have any homework until next Friday. Oh, and I forgot to tell you that we were supposed to have 20 bucks today for the field trip next week, so can you give me 40 bucks right now? Did Linda call here? I've been texting her forever …! Oh, and then a girl in our class got sick during Math. It's not fair! Do I have to take Math again next year? It's sooooo boring and like I'm ever gonna need that so what's the point … So when I say I'm not feeling well, the teacher won't let me leave, but she got to go to the nurse's office for the whole rest of the class. So can I go to the mall right now, I can just get something to eat there when I get hungry, cause I'm meeting my friends …"

Green: "Not much, it was fine."

Chapter Nine

Self-esteem and Stress

When we live life in harmony with our Colors, we learn to value and appreciate ourselves in new and powerful ways. Bosses, parents, family and friends all contribute, but true feelings of self-worth and a healthy self-esteem come from within. What we do and how we behave is key, as is a sense of belonging and feeling valued. Self-esteem is not dependent on the regard or esteem of others, but on how we perceive our own acts, behaviors, accomplishments and contributions to the world.

When we live our lives in ways that make us feel both joyful and valuable, we are well on the road to building a positive sense of self. Our self-esteem grows and strengthens with each obstacle we successfully overcome, with each accomplishment we make and every time we touch the lives of others in positive ways.

"Don't undermine your self-worth by comparing
yourself with others. It is because we are
different that each of us is special."
Nancye Sims

No matter our Colors, we all strive to live our lives in ways which help us grow. We all want that, "I'm on top of the world" feeling, all day, everyday. That feeling, like when our job doesn't feel like work because we're doing what we love. When nothing gets us down. When annoyances are minor and obstacles seem easy to tackle. When the lows are not really low. When things just seem to get better and better. When we live as authentic and purposeful a life as possible, mindful of our Colors and ourselves, our self-esteem can not help but grow. It's how we feel about ourselves, no matter what anyone else thinks. It's a self-respect we've earned.

Blue self-esteem grows when they help others, when they feel as if they've made the world a little softer, a little more caring and compassionate. When Blues find opportunities for team-building in the office, when they have coffee with a friend who needs to talk, or volunteer their time and talents, their days become a lot brighter and more meaningful.

Gold self-esteem is linked to their deep-seated sense of duty and responsibility. Being of service, as part of a team, a committee, or a group, and contributing their organizational and planning skills, makes them feel as if they've done what was required – something necessary and worthwhile. When Golds know they are organized and prepared, and when their plans are on track and unfolding the way they envisioned, they breathe a little easier – and feel a little better about themselves.

Green self-esteem comes from true self-knowledge, understanding and success. Their constant search for information and intellectual enlightenment means they focus on the big picture. They place great value on learning, and often look for opportunities to share their knowledge with others. Greens value their logical thought processes and calm demeanors and rely on their analytical abilities. When they combine their many skills to find a solution when everyone else has given up, they are filled with feelings of great joy and satisfaction.

Oranges believe their self-esteem benefits when they've had a fun and successful day, one in which they've successfully managed multiple tasks and projects – all at the same time. They love the thrill of the sale, the chance to think on their feet, and direct, hands-on involvement. Putting out fires and dealing with immediate, critical problems does not create stress for them, but rather the opposite – the adrenaline is what keeps them going and makes them successful.

Oranges love being the center of attention. They feel compelled to use their creative talents to try and find practical solutions for almost any challenge or obstacle. Being busy, being involved and being productive results in happiness and fulfillment.

"Never be content with someone else's definition of you.
Instead, define yourself by your own beliefs, your own
truths, your own understanding of who you are, and
how you came to be. And never be content until
you are happy with the unique person you are!"
Author unknown

Measuring Success

Colors allows each of us the opportunity to discover and honor our own unique strengths and understand what makes each of us feel successful. Whether success is achieved through a specific happening, or comes as a result of a lifetime of specific behavior, each Color has a very different definition. It may be simple – completing a daily to-do list or making a big sale – or it may be harder to measure – making a difference in someone's life – but achieving it is meaningful and important for every Color.

Blues feel successful if they've spent the day listening to the needs of a friend, helping their team or serving clients, and knowing in their heart that they have made a small difference. While there may be times when Blues reflect and think, "I should have done more," this is often the result of their measuring themselves against another Color's definition of achievement and success. Blues will always be about quality over quantity. They take the time to build meaningful relationships with clients. Trouble comes when a different Color boss looks only at the length of their call times or the small number of appointments they have set. If their boss does not see the value in the loyalty and relationships that have been created, then there can be serious consequences.

Our values, what makes us feel good about ourselves and the world, may be very different than those set by society, our employers, or even our partners. It is vitally important that we measure ourselves using only our own criteria, ignoring other voices and other Colors' definitions. Choosing to tally our successes on our own personal scales is the foundation on which we build positive self-esteem.

Whatever your Color, you must start with a positive attitude and an appreciation for your own successes. Focusing on others' definitions of achievement – at the expense of our own Color's definition – leads to stress, unhappiness, and low self-esteem.

Running on Empty

When your world has been turned upside down, when there is disharmony and conflict in your family or workplace, when it seems as if you experience anger, hurt, prejudice and insults on a daily basis, when you feel excluded and unloved, or when you feel as if you just don't know who you are anymore, it makes sense that your self-esteem and feelings of self-worth will suffer.

Feelings of low self-esteem may be directly related to feelings of stress, but remember that stress is defined differently for each Color, and just as different things contribute to building self-esteem depending on your Colors, so do different things contribute to lowering your self-esteem depending on your Colors. In fact, something which brings one Color great joy and builds their self-esteem may have the exact opposite effect on another Color.

Oranges love to multi-task and be crazy-busy. They avoid boredom at all costs and crave variety and the adrenaline rush that comes from being under the gun. For Golds, having many things that need to be done at once, adding more and more items to the list – while finishing and crossing off nothing – creates huge amounts of stress. Finishing tasks results in positive feelings of self-worth for Golds, while Oranges just crave one more thing to do.

If we understand what contributes, specific to our Colors, to our feelings of low self-esteem and self-worth, then we may be able to avoid the triggers and counteract the effects. Reducing our exposure to certain stressors, and becoming more aware of our own warning signs, will lead us to a better and deeper understanding of ourselves and others. After all, we cannot change or heal what we do not acknowledge or understand.

Blue

Blues who are experiencing low self-esteem often act in uncharacteristic ways. Blues have a tendency to neglect their own needs in order to take care of others, avoiding their own issues and situations. If this goes on for too long, they may start to feel that nobody cares about – or cares for – them. They may start questioning whether they really are doing enough for others. They may cry more easily, and for longer periods of time. When Blues reach overload, sometimes things just blow up.

Low self-esteem means Blues feel as though no one loves them. Couple this with their difficulty in asking for anything for themselves and their inability to say no, and things become really troubling, and their low self-esteem may manifest through anger.

Anger turned inward may sometimes become depression. Before verbalizing their feelings, many Blues try to suppress them. In this state, food may become their only friend and source of comfort, the end result of which may be weight gain and increasing feelings of self-doubt as they hide from the world and ignore their feelings.

Blues in this state, having catered to the wishes of others for so very long, may become selfish, passive-aggressive, or they may withdraw altogether.

Blues experiencing low self-esteem may:

act phony-nice

become judgmental

cry

feel numb, and shut down

feel useless

have trouble making decisions

over-eat, or eat very little

feel overwhelmed by problems

withdraw, avoiding people

feel anxious

blame others

drop out

exhibit extreme people-pleasing behaviors

develop a get-even mind-set

lose their reasoning skills

over-react

become vindictive

seem more aggressive

Gold

Golds' usual calm, concerned manner visibly changes when they have low self-esteem. They over-plan and over-prepare and exhibit signs of anxiety, stress, and worry. Their ever-present drive to do more, and to do better, means that even in those times when they feel positive they can be hard on themselves. When their feelings of self-worth are low, they turn their expectations outward, and offer those closest to them criticism, an attitude of impatience and harsh judgments. Their black-or-white world view becomes even more defined, and their behavior becomes more rigid.

Golds like to get things done – it's all about closure. But when they are not feeling good about themselves, Golds may simply quit, adopting a "what's the use?" and "what's the point?" attitude. This applies to their personal relationships as well as to their work. They just want their troubles to be over, and if that means they have to quit or walk away, then so be it. Over-reacting and self-destructive behaviors don't matter – they need to be done and need to move forward.

When things become really bad, Golds often avoid others, relying only on themselves. They may take on more and more work, which makes things worse, of course. Other signs that things are not as they should be include feelings of fatigue and depression, wanting to hide at home, in bed, until everything has gone away. When Golds are overwhelmed, they tend to reflect on how much they have done for others and rewrite history to focus on how little help and cooperation they received in return. Golds with low self-esteem may feel sorry for themselves and seek sympathy from others.

Golds experiencing low self-esteem may:

seem abrupt and short-tempered

appear confrontational

be defensive and blame others

follow rules blindly

become workaholics

lose sleep

make others feel guilty or lazy

micro-manage others

feel that nobody does anything right

feel that they are not doing enough

over-perfect and over-prepare

work only to "good enough"

stress over little things

adhere to strict schedules

see only faults and problems

have no tolerance for getting off-track

Orange

If Oranges can't find positive, constructive ways to satisfy their need for adrenaline rushes and constant excitement, they may engage in risk-taking behavior. Oranges' feelings of low self-esteem and self-worth may manifest themselves in alcohol and drug abuse, or compulsive gambling. These temporary substitutes may cause Oranges to act out or exhibit rude, uncharacteristic behaviors. They may lash out, purposely breaking rules and policies. Their physical energy can even escalate into violence.

Oranges with low self-esteem may experience overwhelming feelings of anger, and this anger is often turned outward. Oranges may use information they have about someone against them, lashing out and being hurtful. They may also avoid making decisions, procrastinating and going against their "make it happen" nature. Conversely, they may make a snap decision, simply walking away from their relationship or their job, dealing with the consequences after the fact.

Oranges with low self-esteem may:

procrastinate and avoid decisions

engage in hit-and-run arguments

use inappropriate humor

not honor commitments

use put-downs and cheap shots

roll their eyes

feel they need to, "get them before they get me"

forgive but never resolve

think "who cares?"and "whatever"

have a "just kidding" attitude

use physical intimidation

seek revenge

enjoy rubbing it in

Green

It's sometimes hard to know when Greens are in trouble. Their usual attitude is calm, cool and collected, so low self-esteem may be difficult to detect. It is often manifested through sarcastic, sharp, or judgmental comments. While Greens are known for their extensive vocabulary and sharp wit, during these times, their comments can be particularly damaging.

Greens who are questioning their self-worth will likely withdraw further, becoming even quieter and more guarded. They may be stubborn, refusing to cooperate with anyone about anything. Their critical bent becomes even more exaggerated. At these times, Greens may begin second-guessing past decisions, re-thinking and re-evaluating past events.

This over-analysis can stymie current projects, putting Greens in a state where they are not capable of making any decision, where they can not move forward because they are too concerned with looking back. Or they may focus exclusively on one issue, which becomes all-consuming.

Greens with low self-esteem may:

always need more information	seem condescending
be overly cynical or sarcastic	feel defensive
need to be right	be unable to make decisions
have a low frustration level	need more and more alone time
over-think and over-analyze	ask rapid-fire questions
shut down and withdraw	act stubborn and entrenched
experience waves of second-guessing	need to prove, "I'm right"

All of us know when we have reached our limit, but knowing the early warning signs may help us before we get there – before the trouble starts. With every Color, when self-esteem is low, certain stressor may trigger drastic reactions.

An excellent Gold bar manager for a well-known restaurant chain was responsible for huge increases in volume during his first year. While he worked with a large group of Orange staff, he was able to keep his "right" way of organizing the bar in check and under control. But when someone went into "his" tool drawer for the third time and didn't return a hammer to the "right" place, he lost it. The scene he made about something so trivial actually got him fired.

Professional football player Terrell Owens' career offers us another example of an Orange exhibiting extreme and drastic reactions. Owens believed that not enough attention was paid to him after his touchdown receptions. At one point he went public – very public – with his displeasure, lashing out at his teammates. Shortly afterwards, the Philadelphia Eagles suspended Owens and subsequently traded him to the Dallas Cowboys, who also gave up on him.

The symptoms and behaviors which point to low self-esteem are really cries for help. We are all a unique combination of Colors, so the general guidelines set forth here are just that – guidelines. Many actions and behaviors overlap, or manifest themselves in different ways depending on your primary Color. There are a number of books and seminars that may be helpful in the short term, but when the behavior persists, it's time to find a professional. Low self-esteem can be countered quickly, but even if it's an on going, chronic situation, help is available. Find it.

Chapter Ten

The Last Word

There is no better or worse Color. There is no right or wrong combination. There is no team or office that would be more successful if there were only three more of this Color, or two less of that one. Every combination of Colors is the ideal combination for a relationship, because love is Colorblind.

It all starts with an open heart, an open mind and an understanding of ourselves, our friends, and our loved ones through Colors. Now we can begin to spend more time celebrating what we have in common instead of focusing on our differences. It is time, finally, to value and appreciate the positives and the blessings of each of our Colors.

The Colors of the World

Once upon a time the Colors of the world started to quarrel. All claimed that they were the best, the most important, the most useful.

Green said, "Clearly I am the most important. I am the sign of life and of hope. I was chosen for grass, trees, and leaves. Without me, all animals would die. Look over the countryside and you will see that I am in the majority."

Blue retorted, "You only think about the earth, but consider the sky and the sea. It is the water that is the basis of life and drawn up by the clouds from the deep sea. The sky gives space and peace and serenity. Without my peace, you would all be nothing."

Yellow chuckled: "You are all so serious. I bring happiness and warmth into the world. The sun is yellow, the moon is yellow, and the stars are yellow. Every time you look at a sunflower, the whole world starts to smile. Without me there would be no joy."

Orange started next to blow her trumpet. "I am the color of health and strength. I may be scarce, but I am precious for I serve the needs of human life. I carry the most important vitamins. Think of carrots, pumpkins, oranges, mangoes, and papayas. I don't hang around all the time, but when I fill the sky at sunrise or sunset, my beauty is so striking that no one gives another thought to any of you."

And so the Colors went on boasting, each convinced of his or her own superiority. Their quarreling became louder and louder. Suddenly there was a startling flash of bright lightening, and thunder rolled and boomed. Rain started to pour down relentlessly. The Colors crouched down in fear, drawing close to one another for comfort.

In the midst of the clamor, rain began to speak. "You foolish Colors, fighting amongst yourselves, each trying to dominate the rest. Don't you know that you were each made for a special purpose, unique and different? Join hands with one another and come to me."

Doing as they were told, the Colors united and joined hands. The rain continued, "From now on, when it rains, each of you will stretch across the sky in a great bow of color as a reminder that you can all live in peace. So whenever a good rain washes the world, and a Rainbow appears in the sky let us remember to appreciate one another."

Author unknown

Your Beautiful Picture

Have you ever received a picture from a young child? It's usually a picture torn out of a coloring book, with vivid colors scrawled all over the page, in and out of the lines.

Our expressions at receiving such a gift often range into wonder rather than simple thanks. We are thrilled at the heartfelt gift and recognize that one day this picture will change. More colors will be added, patterns will develop, but no picture later will please us any more than this gift we've just been given.

You see, God doesn't expect a perfect picture and He doesn't expect you to understand it fully, or to use every color He has created. He couldn't care that you drew inside the lines or not, and He will always understand that special scrawl in the corner drawn just for Him. He could not be more pleased, and He could not love it any more. Each of our lives is that picture to God – that rough and unique gift that each of us draws very differently.

We never consider that our young friend is upset that their picture isn't perfect. That they could have made us just a little more pleased if their picture had more technique. Don't ever beat yourself up over a part of your life you thought you could have done better. Don't ever consider hiding it from Him that created you entirely as you are.

All we have to do to make God happy is to give Him our gift as it is – as we are. He understands that we do not have the perfect picture and that we will not always succeed, but He simply asks that we try and accept our picture just as we drew it.

Sarah Rudd

A Note From the Author

Anyone who has already attended a Colors seminar has experienced first-hand the vast difference between reading a book and living the training. It brings the material to life in three-dimensional ways with tools that last a lifetime. I invite you to make this a goal in your life and with your team for this coming year.

Imagine the positive changes if everyone simply understood us a little better, with the tools and knowledge to speak our language, celebrate our differences, and value us just the way we are.

George J. Boelcke, CCP
www.vantageseminars.com

About the Author

George Boelcke, CCP is President of Vantage Consulting. As author, speaker, and frequent media guest, he facilitates seminars on personality types, relationships, sales, and team-building throughout North America and Europe for groups ranging from Fortune 500 companies to conferences, sales teams and church groups.

George is the bestselling author of: *The Colors of Relationships*, *Colors Tools for Christians*, *The Colors of Leadership and Management*, and *The Colors of Sales and Customers*.

The Colors Self-Assessment

Score each group of words, for all eight questions, on a scale of:

  4 – which is the most like you

  3 – which is quite a bit like you

  2 – which is a little bit like you

  1 – which is the least like you

  (Each question can have only one score of 1, one 2, one 3 and one 4.)

1. a) _____ compassion, sharing, sympathetic

 b) _____ duty, detailed, traditions

 c) _____ verbal, risk-taker, promoter

 d) _____ rational, knowledge, visionary

2. a) _____ feelings, meaningful, cooperation

 b) _____ conservative, reliable, stability

 c) _____ spontaneous, generous, action

 d) _____ credibility, focused, probing

3. a) _____ authentic, encouraging, spiritual

 b) _____ devoted, cautious, status quo

 c) _____ surprises, freedom, shortcuts

 d) _____ inventive, principled, competence

4. a) _____ unique, sensitive, peacemaker

 b) _____ steady, planning, loyal

 c) _____ open-minded, playful, hands-on

 d) _____ curious, determined, rational

5. a) ____ tender, involved, connecting
   b) ____ lists, procedural, responsible
   c) ____ competitive, outgoing, direct
   d) ____ exploring, skeptical, complex

6. a) ____ devoted, caring, self-improvement
   b) ____ dependable, structured, belonging
   c) ____ flexible, daring, persuasive
   d) ____ independent, perfectionist, reserved

7. a) ____ intuition, sharing, positive
   b) ____ orderly, honor, rule-follower
   c) ____ immediate, skillful, active
   d) ____ theoretical, calm and cool, learning

8. a) ____ affectionate, accommodating, harmony
   b) ____ private, serious, moral
   c) ____ networking, adventure, winning
   d) ____ analytical, logical, improving

Your total score for:

a) Blue ____ b) Gold ____ c) Orange ____ d) Green ____

(The total of your four scores will equal 80.)